For dear Cindy

Transparent Dreams

AN INDIA JOURNEY

A LYRICAL MEMOIR - SUSAN TAIT CHARMAN

With much affection

Susan

FriesenPress

Suite 300 - 990 Fort St
Victoria, BC, V8V 3K2
Canada

www.friesenpress.com

ISBN

978-1-4602-9005-7 (Hardcover)
978-1-4602-9006-4 (Paperback)
978-1-4602-9007-1 (eBook)

1. BIOGRAPHY & AUTOBIOGRAPHY, PERSONAL MEMOIRS

Distributed to the trade by The Ingram Book Company

TABLE OF CONTENTS

Black Notebook (1988–1990)

1990

FOREWORD

It had never once occurred to me to go to India. I think maybe I thought it was a fairy tale place, like my feeling about Timbuktu. To me, places of stories, romanticized, mysterious and so far away that there was no reasonable possibility to actually go there.

Naive.

But then, in 1974, my brother moved away.

To India.

We are close in age, had been close as young children, and our lives became divergent as we grew. He had been a student, mathematics, physics, and was on a spiritual search. I was not. I was a young working wife and became a mother the very month that he went away. We were at different junctures.

John had been corresponding with "The Mother" in Pondicherry, Tamil Nadu, India.

I can't speak for him, because this is my story, but he clearly was pulled to the spirituality, the philosophy of Her and Sri Aurobindo which drew him to the Sri Aurobindo Ashram in Pondicherry, and then to Auroville.

He sent letters, those wonderful blue airmail folded pages. They were brief, esoteric, and far apart. Mail in those days took weeks to reach in each direction, if it arrived at all.

My son grew, marriage dissolved (we are now friends), I evolved in directions that were channelling me also toward Auroville.

Still with no intention of going to India herself, John became a magnet.

I wrote to the Indian Embassy in Ottawa. Please would they send me posters. I was using every fibre of determination to visualize actually pulling off this dream. It was in the mid-80's. The world seemed so huge to me. They did send a tube of beautiful posters, and I put them all over my house, where they would be in my field of vision wherever I looked: from my bed, the bath, hallway, kitchen. I had a series of dreams, vignettes of reconnecting, homecomings. I worked very hard and earned enough to free myself for a year. Still with no plan except: GET TO JOHN.

September 6, 1986, I stepped off the edge of my known world.

****

Here, from the Auroville website directly, is an explanation of Auroville, and it's Charter.

Auroville was born on 28 February 1968.

Its founder, the Mother, created the Auroville Charter consisting of four main ideas which underpinned her vision for Auroville. When Auroville came into being, All India Radio (AIR) broadcast the Charter, live, in 16 languages. Aurovilians apply the ideas of the Auroville Charter in their daily life, in policy-development, and decisions, big and small. The Charter thus forms an omnipresent referent that silently guides the people who choose to live and work for Auroville.

The Auroville Charter

Auroville belongs to nobody in particular. Auroville belongs to humanity as a whole. But, to live in Auroville, one must be a willing servitor of the divine consciousness.

Auroville will be the place of an unending education, of constant progress, and a youth that never ages.

Auroville wants to be the bridge between the past and the future. Taking advantage of all discoveries from without and from within, Auroville will boldly spring towards future realisations.

Auroville will be a site of material and spiritual researches for a living embodiment of an actual human unity.

www.auroville.org.in

SETTING OUT

October 1986

From the sailboat Raven, letter to my parents

I salute your braveness in opening your arms to let me go. It was difficult to watch you both watch me as I stepped onto the boat to become out of reach. Dad's arm around you, his last words, "Go get your brother and bring him back." I will try. Everyone at home becomes some sort of an emotional anchor.

This seems a funny way to get to India, but the feeling of the importance of the journey itself has been so strong that I've chosen to crew on a sailboat part of the way on my path to reach my only brother. My little brother. He's been gone for twelve years, leaving on his quest the same month that my son was born. This is the first moment that I'm free enough to follow. I am unsure of my reception on the other side of the ocean, but am on my way.

I knew when we left that we might not make it—that I might become invisible out there, or drown. We didn't have a motor—oh, we did, but it didn't work. All for show—pure sailing.

Victoria
Port San Luis Obispo
Channel Islands Harbour
Santa Catalina
San Diego

We've been together for weeks now, through storms, near death, grand adventures, bonded almost to a marriage. It's time for me to make the leap for India. The captain of another boat, together with my boys, commandeered a truck to get us to the nearest airport. We are highly emotional as we near. Another leaving.

I'm the last to board the plane, a rush across the tarmac to the waiting stewardesses at the bottom of the stairway. I turn and see my crew standing still, not moving. I run back and fling myself into their arms for one more goodbye. I see through my tears that everyone is smiling at us. A good farewell.

The flight is long, but I've been on this journey for thirty-eight years—it's all right.

Madras

John is there, actually there, to meet me. An amazement to see him after all these years, to meet successfully at a tiny point of time and space. It's late in the night, and dark. We have more travelling to do. Several hours to somewhere—I've only a vague idea where it is on a map. The air is warm and enveloping, moist and fragrant, mysterious, a blur of another world. We talk, snooze in the taxi, talk some more. The distance is bridged, the years dissolve. I have arrived. Along the road there are small pools of light that turn into tea shops. We stop. The glee of it all, tea in the night.

Still in the dark we arrive in Auroville. I am installed in the Guest House. Soft tones of settling me and he will be there again in the morning.

Daylight and birdsong. Tropical trees and flowers, new scents and sounds. All new. Still like a dream.

We breakfast under a banyan tree in the garden, and straight away John takes me to the centre of Auroville. Both the physical and spiritual middle—the Matrimandir. We climb and climb all the way up and through to the very top of the roof, where I can see all around, to the sea on one horizon and hard red desert interspersed with a green I've never seen before on the other. My new home. We descend gradually to the outstretched hands of a sari'd Indian woman. She takes my hands in hers and, looking into my eyes, says, "I think you should stay." My heart catches her words.

A Low Granite Castle
October 1986

A low granite castle—not a palace—a fortress castle in the garden. A hundred dinner guests mill throughout. I slip away in the dusk and wander through the trellised terrace toward the solitude of the lotus-covered pool beyond. And dive in cleanly.

And wake, still drenched in the dream.

The prince appears without warning. I first hear his voice. Melodiously deep and foreign above my head, asking my brother how long would I be there. Turning, I am startled by the electric blue shock of his eyes. I am faint with recognition—my *mate* of centuries. I see so deeply I am afraid I do not recognize his surface and he will be lost again.

Desiderio—a name of longing, desire...

16 November 86

My birthday has come within three weeks of arriving in India. My first birthday in Auroville. A full day, a full moon day in November.

In the early morning, before breakfast, we leave the Guest House. We, five women, paths intercepting, bonded just because of that. We cycle through the relative cool of dawn, through rice fields and a corridor of royal palms to the ancient temple of Ilaingarkal.

Instantly we are surrounded by a raggedy cı. village children. Fascinated by us, the eldest boy sep. himself, approaches me, and asks with little English if I would like a lotus from the pond. Yes.

As I watched in open-hearted wonder, he stripped off his *lungi* and plunged. I catch the moment with my shutter as he rises from the water, pink lotus poised in his hand. Diving again, he comes back to me, arms full of the magnificent blooms. I see his shy return and think, how nice—he's bringing one for each of us. But no, he has somehow caught the glow of my birthday and gives them all to me.

Sunk. Caught again by the magic in the air. I cry and cry.

Breakfast—a tea party lasting till noon. With my dear long-lost brother so close, with cake, and more flowers.

Evening
16 November 86

A gift to me—from me.

On birthdays, it seems, there is a special dispensation to ask for what you want. John, my almost-twin, delivers me to Desiderio. The path unwinds through tropical gardens to a closely surrounded clearing; the fortress castle appears.

In the presence of his exotic intensity I am frightened, nervous, unsure. He makes me hot chocolate, gifts me a journal of his poetry, formally gives me his friendship. And the offer of his extra house. The lotus pond dream resurfaces, foreshadowing the depth of his invitation.

Letters Home
2 November 86

I want to write to everyone but there are too many things to tell you.

1. I am here safely.

2. John is alive and well.

We tried today to reserve telephone calls for tomorrow. If we get through you will know. The phone at the Guest House isn't working at all. The one at Matrimandir quit while John was on it.

This place is almost beyond description and maybe that's why John's letters have been so ethereal. I've been taking all the pictures I dare (monsoon season—I leave the camera home if I'm going out too long). I'm also not sure yet what is an intrusion and what isn't.

Already I'm almost taking John for granted and that's what you're waiting to hear. What it boils down to: this seems to be his home now, and a wonderful one. It has its share of problems, as does anywhere, but it's basically an appealing and exciting place to be. I've been told that this isn't really the real India—that Auroville just happens to be here and I understood that from what I read before coming.

But there can no longer be any forgetting or pretending I'm anywhere near home. This place is foreign; it IS India.

John has been taking me on little tours every day, to different parts of Auroville. We started out walking (and climbing) to the top of Matrimandir, which looks exactly like its pictures except that it was impossible to tell before just what a central part of the community it is. He has introduced me to countless people, all of whom were expecting me—many knew details of my trip. Some said, "We have been waiting for you." It was comforting to find out that he was really looking forward to my arrival. Also to see how much the people here care about him. In his quiet, gentle way I think John is a leader here. "King of the Workshop" is what someone said to me. You would get a kick out of watching him speaking Tamil with the "boys," cheerfully getting things done.

Yesterday was a huge holiday: Diwali, Festival of Lights. Sort of like New Year's and felt like Christmas. John and I had dinner at an Indian friend's house. I felt quite honoured to be there. Very elaborate floral decorations everywhere, candles and a huge great traditional dinner, delicious and too filling. Afterwards, just about the whole of Auroville went to a movie at the auditorium here, a real event because it draws so many people out. It was *The Empire Strikes Back*.

John was excited because it was a science fiction thing; I remember he was always a sucker for that. I was amused at having come all this way to see it for the first time.

We went to the beach today, by motorbike. Shorts and t-shirts, sandals, not a hint of being even cool on the road. Of course, you don't go too fast. Always there are cyclists and bullock carts, cows, goats, people, and puddles.

The beach has Hawaii beat. The water was so comfortable I could have stayed in all day, except we got tired from playing in the waves—trying to bodysurf and diving around for shells. Lots of fishing boats around (unlike home) and tropical, tropical trees and flowers. I will go with my camera after the monsoon in a few weeks.

The flowers are INCREDIBLE. Over one hundred varieties of plumeria, apparently. Hibiscus, gardenia, bougainvillea, roses, orchids, and strange lovely flowers everywhere. People pick them and use them all over the place, anywhere. The Indian girls often have bunches of them tied in their hair, braided at the back. Beautiful.

The houses are INCREDIBLE. John's is rather hobbity— delightful. I have photos.

Tomorrow John and I may make the trip to "Pondy." More excitement. It will take a while even to see all of Auroville because it is so spread out, full of little pockets of activity.

I can tell it will be hard to write home from here, but I will continue to try. It's because every single thing is so different; it's not just a matter of describing the scenery, or the people, or the food, or that you have to sleep under a mosquito net, or boil the milk when it's delivered. You likely won't be able to shut me up for weeks when I get back.

Love from both of us to you all. I hope we will have spoken to you already—we TRIED! As they say, this is India.

Susan

PS: We didn't get through. We think the operator on your end did, but the tie-up is usually from Pondy to Madras. We will try again, but if we don't reach you, the word is that it's easier from your end. Hope it wasn't too frustrating for you if the phone call got halfway.

with love always, Susan

5 November 86

Dear Mom and Dad:

Oh dear, I hope now after the phone call you aren't frustrated and worried. We are choosing to think that you realize that we are FINE; we were just trying to phone as expected. It would be easier if you could call us. Drop a note with the time and date; we can reserve calls. If it's a bad connection, hanging up and having the operator try again is apparently the route to go. We spent a lot of funny time on the line yelling "Hello, hello," just to raise an operator.

I wanted to tell you that John doesn't have quite the accent that comes across on the phone—or maybe it's because I'm already getting used to the hodgepodge of voices around here. At the moment, at the Guest House we represent Holland, Germany, Switzerland, USA (New York and New Mexico), Bombay, and Canada (me). I found out why he sounded so Indian on the phone; it was because of the Indian telephone system, mostly. He does have an accent, but not as pronounced in person. It quite suits him, I think. There is every possible variety of Indian (as well as most every other nationality) here and they are very different from each other, even in appearance, bone structure, and colour.

I am trying to learn enough Tamil to at least be able to make myself a little understood.

Postage IS really comparatively prohibitive. The last letter I sent you cost twelve rupees. You can buy a cotton skirt for eight (at the Sunday market) or a t-shirt for much less. You can have a tailor sew you an outfit for about twenty-five (same or next day). What this also points out is that there doesn't seem to be much or any relation here between time, labour, and the cost of articles. About 12.9 rupees = $1 US. So, it will cost practically nothing for me to pick up a few warm weather clothes. I will be ready for summer in Canada.

I would like to stay until my visa runs out (end of January), at least, with an extension of another three months if possible. There is SO MUCH to see. John and I ventured into Pondy yesterday on the motorcycle. Whole new planet, I think. A mass of human activity. Where we are is very beautiful and peaceful and clean so I will send pictures from here first. John is a great guide and I'm so glad he is here to show the way a little.

Love to you all. I will try to get this in the post so that there is less time for you to worry, if you are.

xox Susan

PS: Birthday card arrived. Thank you.

Thursday
26 November? 86

I just realized that I am near a typewriter with no official work to do. I take that back—someone just walked in with the key. I've walked into transcribing a conference on education that was held here, headed by the minister of education, who was involved with the Sri Aurobindo Ashram and is therefore quite concerned about education in Auroville. It's been a wonderful way to become acquainted with the system here, and also the people involved. Interesting for me, and not terribly tedious. A couple hours in the morning, a couple days a week. There is also to be an international conference on healing here in January. I will send a brochure at some point. It's fascinating; I feel that my timing for this trip is exceptional. I have been asked to help coordinate the information office, which is also not too tedious. I will have "flunkies" and be right in the midst of the whole thing (which, of course, is right where I want to be).

Thank you for taking care of all the mundane details for me. Rewards will come to you. The second parking ticket was never even in my hand—I didn't even see it until I was driving down the highway and then it blew off the windshield; who would believe that?! To boot, I was advised by our infamous lawyer friend to just ignore them and not worry about it because... well, just because. I have no idea what the insurance company is up to, or that dreadful man, the bus driver who hit my car. Imagine that driver of a speeding bus, who hit and destroyed a tiny convertible, thinking that he should sue for loss of sleep! At least we know that the accident wasn't my fault and that, oh yes, I wasn't hurt. I will just have to not worry about it until I get home. Ah, stress from around the world. To be continued...

HAHA: finished! I actually feel privileged to have been allowed to type that information; this machine is something that everyone wants to get their hands on.

Thank you very much for the cheque. It will go VERY far, to a jolly Christmas and beyond. I have written to the woman who bought all my furniture and didn't pay to say that by the time she reads my letter and sends a draft or whatever to me directly, the timing should just about coincide with when I run out of money. I'm not really that desperate, especially now that I am moving next week and money should go about twice as far (it really is amazing here). She did assure me when I spoke to her that the money she owes me would be in the bank at the end of that month (which was October)—maybe not all of it, but some at least. This is not to worry you, but just so that you are aware.

I am sure that our letters have been crossing each other, as they have with John all these years—questions and answers in the air at the same time. One concrete answer: as expected, I'm going to try to extend my tourist visa—which would bring my stay here until the end of April. And then I will head right home.

It's such a joy to spend time with John. Even though I have dived right into life here, we spend part of every day (with the odd exception) together. Doing the tour of Auroville, some walking, some cycling, some motorcycle. Visiting for teas in the late afternoons, dinners and lunches still lined up and waiting for us. We have had people thinking that we are twins. It seems the mannerisms and gestures developed in common as children are still there, and they think we look the same. It is quite fun.

Next week I will move into a house on my own. John's good friend Desiderio, who met him (John) while he was unconscious with hepatitis in the hospital so many years ago, has offered me his mother's house. It's a beautiful spot. Many of the homes here have guesthouses or an extra little place for people to stay. Showers, etc. are normally separate from the main house, and outdoors. It's an enchanting way to have things, with gardens and flowers everywhere. That will cost me 5 Rs/day (which goes to Auroville), and then meals still at the kitchen (where John eats) are...I'm not sure quite how much, maybe 15 Rs/day. Right now there are thirteen rupees per US dollar. Not too bad!

Dad, I'm sorry to hear that you are having a hard time right now. Warm weather does wonders, for sure. You would love it here; it's the same temperature at night whether you are in bed or out of it. Think of me swimming, too, while you are in Hawaii. This is a GOOD place, Dad. It's easy to see why the people here from all over the world have come. I will try to explain when I am home in the spring. Meanwhile, trust that John is well and happy, loved and respected, and doing a lot of very good work. You should be proud of him. I am. I will be bringing home masses of stories—and pictures will arrive before me. I will bring presents when I come. Will you write to me if you have the inclination? Even a card? See you soon.

With love always,

Susan

Tamil Nadu, India 605 101
3 December 86

Greetings!

Best wishes for the New Year. John happily received the stretchy ropes and the Christmas cheque you sent.

Thanks—it will be well-used. I am still well and active. In fact, John says I will need a vacation by the time I finish here!

There, we've equalled things out a bit this Christmas by having John and I together. I hope the rest of you can manage to gather in one spot.

I've just moved out of the Central Guest House to a lovely "private" house, a big change from the crowded guest house.

Have a good trip to Maui.

Think of us while you are sitting close to the fireplace. I trust you got my letter with thank-yous; if not, I send them, also our love.

Always, Susan

12 December 86

Dear Mom and Dad

Oh my God! That sounds like no one has received any letters—and I've been writing like mad. Maybe it's true what they say, that sixty percent of things don't go anywhere. But it works both ways, I suppose. You are the only ones I've heard from except for a postcard from Paris yesterday.

The dictionary sounds like a GREAT idea. I am right now making a lot of use of the French/English one I got a few weeks ago. I'm practising by telling Desiderio anything I have to convey, in written French. We are both enjoying it.

I have been forced to take most of my clothes off, because it's just too warm. Well, not exactly true. You can't go around with no clothes here like at home, but a loose t-shirt and underwear ought to be OK in the house. A nice breeze is blowing and the doors and windows are all open. I may have a small fever. We've survived a bout of flu. John was hit a bit harder than me and is now "damn fine," but I am hit in the kidneys. Nothing to worry about, I'm just telling you. I have been to the doctor.

A friend brought me a spray of delicate little yellow orchids the other day. They're called "dancing ladies"; try to look it up in a book, they are lovely.

I feel so glad to be with John each day I see him. I hope that your Christmas day was as lovely and peaceful as ours.

Congratulations on losing ten pounds! I know a great way to lose more. Come over here! Not everyone loses weight, apparently, but most, including me, do. Bicycling, rice usually twice a day, and just general melting away—and this is supposed to be almost as cold as it gets.

Tomorrow I go to Madras for the day with a friend to pick up one of the lecturers for the Healing Congress: the "Breathing Lady" from Germany. The taxi is paid for. The usual practice is for someone to go up with the taxi and take advantage of the "day in the city" because a round trip is included in the fare and, well, that's just how it's done.

Two days ago I had been here for two months. When I announced it at breakfast at the Guest House, someone said, "Did you say two years?" I said, "Yes, that feels more like it."

Transparent Dreams

It's all so strange. Weeks rush by in a day but each moment within stands still somehow. I don't know how I can explain, or even if I can. I admit that I already feel an ache of missing India—not just John—and I have four more months to be here. It may be partly because of simply not being able to ignore or cover over a single moment. No radio or television or phone. Those things do exist here but are rare.

The air here is different. The sky is different. It's wider, somehow. Some days it's almost a bit too different. Like the other day, when John and I went to Pondicherry on the motorcycle for him to buy steel for the Matrimandir (it was to be picked up later in the *vandi*—bullock cart). I can't even describe it. I've been sitting here for ten minutes trying to think of a way. Maybe you can read the book about Calcutta that I read just before I left: *City of Joy*, I think. Pondy isn't that horrendous (it's a small city), but it's all there—the poverty, the lepers, the colours. Even when I went alone on my cycle the other Sunday and didn't for hours see another white-skinned person, there was no thought of fear—or even being out of place. The Indian people I've encountered appear to have a lovely gracious acceptance of things. We ARE different and they certainly DO notice. But it seems like they feel that even if we Have Come From some Other Planet, it's not an intrusion; we simply are all part of the scheme. It's so nice a feeling and a very good lesson.

Tea time.

I have sent three rolls of film to be mailed from Australia. There will be a much better chance of their arrival from there (or anywhere—that just happened to be the first convenient person in transition). Somewhere I have written a rundown of what is on the film and will send it.

My new camera is acting up—due to climate, I suspect— but I am trusting it's nothing serious, just a matter of having "contacts cleaned." There seem to be people here who can handle most everything.

Responses to my inquiries about a trip to Madras are varied. People do plan shopping trips; there is silk everywhere, apparently.

Tineke, from the Guest House, gave me a list of things she needs and said, "Enjoy the South Indian metropolis."

John: "I took a friend there once and she promptly got typhoid."

Desiderio: "It is the ugliest place imaginable—but maybe it's good that you go—now you won't have to imagine hell anymore," all conveyed with a very dramatic French accent.

I also couldn't help thinking of how Dad resists trips to Vancouver, which is, to start with, one of the most beautiful cities ever. Now that you're settled into the island lifestyle, especially his days have new parameters: never come up from the beach empty-handed, chop and stack firewood, pay attention to each drop of well water, care for the vegetable garden, trim the wicks of the oil lamps, maintain the boat motor and the rowboat to get to and from the fishing boat (anchored in the bay), each evening win the battle with the generator! Why would he want to leave? I am happy to think that after those first few years of pioneering you finally have electricity, and now a telephone.

John and I have just walked home in the dark from hearing an impromptu concert of original music. The nice thing about such an intimate setting is that clapping as a formal appreciation is not necessary; our smiles and laughter and sighs and tears were more than enough.

I will mail this from Madras. Happy New Year! And Happy Hawaii!

with love always,
Susan

January 87

I have been warned never to go out barefoot after dark. The path winds through a grove of plumeria toward the bathroom in the garden. Lit by a little starlight I make my way slowly. And freeze.

My heart is in my throat. I'm dead for sure. My foot has landed on something firm but giving. I wait for the bite. For the pain. Nothing.

I run.

I'm shaking. I'm scared, convinced I've nearly had a stroke. Small-girl-type tears.

In the morning I retrace my steps of the night and come across the hosepipe the gardener has left across the way.

February 87
images of my journey

The sea—with dolphins and whales
with thunder and lightning and calm blue days.

The red earth of India
and her moonlit nights
palm trees and biblical skies above
phoenixes and unicorns

Pink sunrise and orange sunsets
the beach—the desert sand
Cactuses and thorns and
scorpions and snakes
and lotuses, orchids
and roses.

looking back and looking out
Black seas and blacker skies
The dark dark night
Through frightened eyes

Transparent Dreams

We sailed on slowly knowing not
the treacherous course our captain plot
Past midnight crept
the plodding clock,
the hours til dawn
Interminable.

Now I sit on the edge
of India
On the very edge
looking out
waiting for the sun to go down, the stars to come out
It all looks different now
Than before I went to sea.
Even though someone sits
with me
A shawl around us both
pretending we're cold.
Now I can look out
just me
Past the horizon—past seeing the land
And know what is
there.

Sunday afternoon
February 87

We've bicycled back

from the beach

I'm sunburned and showered

Tropical flowered

Up to my fingernails

in henna

Up to my elbows in a

starfruit's juicy ripeness,

There's topaz and turquoise

in my ears

And a deep contentment

That for years and years

was missing

RED CLOTH-BACKED NOTEBOOK

3 February 87 (6:30 a.m.)

I feel so tired. I woke up very early in the night, dreaming about actually arriving home, to the island. Lovely warm welcome, but people trying to hold me in ways that were uncomfortable.

I decided during the day today that when I leave Auroville it will be with a return ticket in my hand.

Sometimes when I get too tired or too many things come at once, I lose my grip on the order of things.

But I've had about enough of having to let go. Remember, though, that this is the only place I've ever sworn I'd return to.

*****

I can be close to you for hours and not want anything more than that. I can fall asleep by your side and be content. A smile from your eyes will make me smile all day. But don't kiss me that way before you go. Because I do want more than that.

Saturday a.m.

Upon awakening, before even moving, I know that whatever force was assaulting me yesterday has lifted, backed off. My ribs are still a little aware of feeling constricted, but I feel lighter. I had described it as being hit by a truck. Was there some great shock that took days to unreel from?

You came and stayed with me both evenings when I was sick, until I was ready to sleep. How can I doubt your sweetness? You just came long enough to bring me a lovely little blue flower, the same colour as the shirt I'm wearing. How can I doubt your love—or change my shirt?

I want to find a way to tell you that I love you—unconditionally. Maybe if I bicycle to Pondy to get cinnamon for your chocolate you will know. Maybe you know already.

In any case, I'll get the cinnamon and then you will know for sure.

*****

I found a way.

I just told you.

Sunday
8 February 87

A difficult painful night.

If anything goes wrong here, it goes totally wrong. Such pain in my ribs I couldn't take a breath, or move. I thought I would have to wait until someone visited me, or hope they did, and have them go for a doctor or my brother.

I am up, still in pain but able to move around. Cleaned my house as well as I could.

The little neighbour girl came. She has crocheted me a belt of beautiful colours.

*****

I am now in the midst of trying to discover something about myself from the photographs I've brought with me.

- observations of my son as he grows
- all the ones of places that I love are taken on the edge, looking out.
- the leaving of the magnificent sailboat, Sid Sirocco, from my west coast island, seemed to be so important. I watched the people who left and those who were left behind. Those who went and those who wanted to go. Less than a year later it was me who slipped out of the berth in Victoria.

John's gone for a nurse; he's right, this isn't a case of indigestion.

Sunday/Monday

Out of commission. Still a small amount of pain tonight but I feel clear and quite strong, though drained. My care-takers have been in and out all day. But I can sleep tonight with no one sitting up with me.

In answer to a question from home: how can the culture not make a difference? How can a country (a new city even) so concerned with its spirituality not have an effect on the moral values? When you are more and more aware of your soul, when love becomes a wider word—a truer and more all-encompassing concept than it usually is in the West—of course things change.

Everything changes. My value of me is elevated.

About this pain

I panic when it grabs me by surprise. I seem to forget so quickly that if I am calm and quiet and sensible, I can win.

Yesterday I felt so much better—I thought.

This morning I needed you to say what you did. There's no escaping it. I have to face every single thing.

I wanted to be held and it seems no human being could do it, so I put a band around my heart and now it's too tight and the more I struggle, the more it locks on.

I cried and cried—tears that felt like they were inside for a long time. Hot tears rolling down my face. I remember the dreams of going home, of magic spells and one of you giving me a beautiful white flower and saying, "If you want to know about love, look at this."

You are here with my brother. I came and found you both, but feel like a clumsy child beside you.

When I left my home, when I left on the boat for here, I knew that one step was going to be on a new path. Now I can't stay here—and I don't fit there because I've started a change and it's bigger than I thought.

When I breathed the soft bright light came between me and the pain and took me away.

Bonds, bindings, only hurt when you stretch against them, when it's time to break through, or release them. If one didn't try to move, you may never even know the ropes were there.

*****

There is a soft slow
lion purr of motorcycles
throbbing into the casuarinas
the heavy drone of the
giant bees
and over and over
the interrupted crescendo
of the brain fever birds.

Morning—it's finally
morning.
I've been in my bed for
days unable to move
or hardly eat or breathe.

People brought me books
I read a little and they lay open
everywhere

Purple orchid flowers
lie wilted, sad because
I couldn't move them
from where they were so sweetly
put.

My caretakers became a little clan
conferring, consulting
questioning
Until last night the black
band of pressure round me
broke, in a great rush of fevered pain.
And I sighed and slept

Sweat pouring from every

pore

Till morning.

This morning.

It's not cool enough to make me shiver or want clothes.

It's the delicious cool of air on my drenched skin when my lover moves.

The old Indian gardener is watching me as I rest on the terrace here in the dappled shade. I watch him too, sometimes, and try to imagine his life.

*****

Each time I glance at our hands, they are usually such a tangle—I can't always tell right away which are my own.

And I nearly always have to let you go so quickly. I feel wrong somehow that I want to keep you near—that I want to hold you closer, longer.

I let you go so easily because I love you, because I know how instantly prison-like not letting go can be.

But please please, don't kiss me on the neck like that.

OK, if this is something I'm supposed to be learning about. Restraint—peace—calm, then put me this close to the most sweet and attractive man I have ever met, make sure that I love him and that it grows each day.

Valentine's Day
14 February 87

Now I've been here through:

Halloween, my birthday, American Thanksgiving, Christmas, New Year's, and soon the Mother's birthday and Auroville's birthday.

Quand je respire comme tu dit, la lumière douce et brillant venu entre moi et la souffrance. Je ne désire pas que tu as vu ces larmes. Elles juste tombe.

10 February 87

Thank you for your sweet patience while I was showing so much weakness. I love you for that.

Pour ta douce patience quand je montre si faiblesse, je t'aime. Il est pas quelque chose d'ordinaire, quelque chose que je peux désirer, mais jamais demander.

Morning
15/16 February

I try for endless patience—endless giving. After all, if patience has an end, it is not truly patience.

17 February 87

Living near you in the garden is like being given the grace to live in the territory of a sweet wild thing.

For twelve years—good or bad—I lived with a man as husband.

For four years since that span, I have stayed part of the time with close friends and the past two years quite alone. I do like very much to be by myself, but the odd time I weaken and feel lonely.

Taking privacy and consideration into account, of course, if I don't feel at ease to come and go also in a friendship, then what is there? I feel my trust misused.

I suppose I should feel amazed that these people gave me as much as they did—as much as they could.

You can't be as sweet and giving in the way you are and expect not to have some effect. I would almost rather you had remained aloof and I were just a little frustrated at the proximity of you.

What I feel—what I can't say to you—is about feeling restraint, feeling that I should not want to make love to you, that I am trying to be detached so that I will still love you— when you don't want me near you.

I also didn't tell you about the dream—of letting go of my hand each time someone came near, which hurt me so much. I don't want or need someone holding me the whole time, but I refuse to be in a position where I am automatically put aside because another friend is there. Notwithstanding, of course, consideration of normal feelings.

It's not a game and there's nothing wrong. It's just a little hard trying to find a balance. Having grown to have you be a part of my life, I like to see you—I like to spend time with you. I feel happy and peaceful when you are near, but because I'm still human sometimes it's not so easy to overlook the physical nearness of you. I guess I need time too.

If you ask that of someone who loves you and want your friendship to continue then patience is called for on both sides.

24 February 87

Letter to my mentor friend

Now it's just over eight weeks until I fly. Remember what we went through before I left on my journey? We'll never forget that horrible time, realizing the treacherous bonds of attachment. The painfulness of impending separation: "You can't hurt me by going away; I will become angry and shut you out first." Of course we do. We'll never forget—and after that, in a milder form, I started to shut down too, but something sparked and I recognized the anger and frustration and now I feel my heart crushing again.

None of these feelings compare with the pain of thinking you and I were no more you and I. Maybe that was preparation and grounding to give us strength. And maybe we will remember the pain of our struggle in time to help us through. You give me strength even across this enormous distance.

Thank you.

love to you, Susan

*****

I have a problem with you and what it boils down to is this: you are not being fair; don't kiss me like that. You are upsetting my equilibrium.

Even a monk who is long-practiced and entrenched in celibacy would have trouble resisting you.

If that's what you truly want, great—it's happily being one of the bigger challenges I've faced and all that I have said to you is truthful.

But don't kiss me like that.

27 February 87

Journey to Pondy: cycling home alone after lunch with a neighbour, talking only about death (the death of her husband),

I am met on the road. "Your brother is looking for you"; my father is dead.

That's what the black band was about—the same symptoms at the same time.

My father has died—

I will have to go

And come back.

1 March 87

Dear Mom,

I will arrive back probably a few days after you get this, and will be free to be company for you if you want. Whatever you need from me you can have.

I know my sisters, your other daughters, are there with you.

I am to the point of counting the weeks, almost the days, steeling myself for the wrench of leaving this place, so John and I agreed simply that the time is best now. Our bond is so secure that you will feel his presence and love with me when I get there; I am sure of it.

The hot season is starting to get underway, warmer every day (soon warm will be a laughable understatement). Time to go.

This week I will make my travel arrangements. Your loan will cover my ticket, did you know that? And I will find a way to let you know, or else I will just be there.

with love always from your Susan, also from John

1 March 87

Last night I dreamed that you and I were walking and went by a lake and saw some small fishes just breaking the surface. You said you would show me how to get them out of the water—just wait, you told me—you dove into the water. Sort of cartwheeled in so smoothly and then kicked up the whole surface of the water from below.

At first it seemed as if nothing was happening but then I saw the shapes coming toward me and then a fish swam right out of the water, right into my waiting hands.

2 March 87

Last night the dreams—today the change in plans.

Plumeria

Frangiapani

Temple Flowers

Psychological Perfection

The January/February calendar page, before always the dark months, now from bonfire to bonfire: New Year's Day to the Mother's Birthday to Auroville's Birthday.

Please, give me a dream to show me the way, clearly and with no pain. Should I be letting go of making decisions, because "It is out of my hands, anyway," or taking responsibility for my own life?

3 March 87
Tuesday holiday lunch

With the chipped ochre walls and garlanded Ganeshes and black plastic tablecloths and bamboo chairs and Desiderio looking like a painting against it all, the old Vellakara at the next table the only other patron in the dingy little Chinese restaurant in the French quarter of Pondicherry. So fallen into his royal blue eyes, so caught by the sweet low murmuring of his voice, so thrown back into her own intimate memories, that she couldn't help but speak to him as we left.

I felt her ache as we gathered our things to go—as I knew she waited for the roar of the motorcycle,

Tearing open an old wound—making the pain fresh.

March 87

You go beyond thinking and feeling. You are a companion of my soul, of me.

Saturday
7 March 87

The last week: two more Sundays at the beach with the girls, how many more sleeping chocolates under the moon or in my house—my house?

Can a Pondicherry travel agent actually materialize something as concrete as an airline ticket?

I haven't cried for two days.

*****

Being able to focus on one thing at a time to choose the depth of field—to choose the timing, the light. The last few days I've been having visions of things swimming into focus, like a flower in the nursery, with my eyes closed.

Sunday morning

Sweet soft sunlight pours into my house. I woke up as the sunrise released the fragrance of the jasmine garland at the foot of my bed, spilling out of the orange clay dish around the crystals and the stone lotus and the candleholder beneath the Mother's picture watching over it all, us all.

I felt the simple joy of being a small girl as I waited for my friends to come so we could bicycle to the beach. I knew that each of them had wanted to go alone with me, but they were able to rise above that and be happy that we could all go. We made a fine happy group. They plotted aloud to go every Sunday without me to the beach to make me jealous and return. But it only made me happy that they would think to do that—and also that they found delight in each other.

*****

Your relationship with my brother may be a little different because of the added dimension of me. Already you have changed your time spent together. It has been seldom if ever alone. Now I get to see each of you alone but you only see each other with me. Now I told him that you said I could come back to this house and then you took my hand, at dinner, with him.

I imagine he doesn't know exactly what to think—or do. After all, he loves us both—and I love both of you.

> When I come back I shouldn't always
> be there in the middle of your time
> together. Sometimes, but not always.

Tell him he hasn't lost a friend. His sister came to town.

10 March 87

Ten days left.

11 March 87

Encashment certificate day: it seems there is a crush of westerners trying to make actual currency and certificates match up. Help from all quarters. Theoretically solved by noon.

"Be fearless and resolute—all obstacles will melt away before you."

-the Mother

Both of us trying for purity. I guess if it weren't a bit of a struggle it wouldn't be a higher thing. And because I am so conscious of aspiring for that...

Why are you so close to me?

Wednesday
11 March

When my plane was going to go on Sunday, my brother said he would go with me to the airport. I wanted to ask you to come and hold my hand. But I think I should go alone. It's all simply too much.

What an incredibly beautiful sound—

Rain.

*****

Do you think being physically close is all right as long as you don't actually make love? Where do you think that line is? It's partly because when you are there for hours—and you are there and then you just pull away, all of a sudden, it's almost too much. I was going to ask you to come to Madras, but I think firstly it's too much to ask of you (I already feel indebted to you) and also it maybe be completely too much for me.

Maybe I should just go alone and leave Auroville in Auroville.

Either you don't feel anything, or you are just trying to make the yoga harder.

*****

You have given me nothing but a peaceful joy; you constantly reaffirm the possibility of the sweetness of man. You are a reflection of my aspirations and so I love you.

The lower things are easy because you can fall into them. The higher ones require a reach—a stretch that we can't always attain on the first attempt. But the attempt is the thing.

13 March 87

One week left. Noon next Friday the plane goes.

It's quite warm—my skin is damp all the time—any exertion at all and it's wet.

15 March

Sunday again, early again. We had the full moon; just more heat, and some drama.

6:00 a.m.

The world is long up—sun is rising, moon is going down.

It's too hot for the beach; it's time to stay home, put my house in order. If there were an airplane today I would go. It's too hot, I'm too tired, there's anguish in the air that I'm having a hard time rising above. To find the calm peacefulness inside myself is the only way. It's the only possible way. How do you go from India with no struggle? Surrender. Be glad of the spring on the other side of the world. Just pack your things and physically be ready to go.

The spirit doesn't need to pack—or worry. There is no need for worry at all. I have viable plans, alternatives, and plasticity.

8:55 p.m.

A friend came, just in time this afternoon. She could see the shock of my leaving taking effect, shrivelling me into a corner. Tea with honey, Bach Flower Rescue Remedy, and the words of a real friend echo in my mind. We reassure each other. Laugh and cry a little, swear to install telephones when I come back. I let her go; my sense of time has returned to normal.

Earlier I had thought I would scream at the seconds taking so long. How would I endure the next four days? I felt I knew what it was to be in prison for eternity.

We walked hand in hand to dinner, both measuring the steps and counting the days. Our arrival did not go unnoticed.

Tomorrow will be for my brother.

Tonight I sleep.

Monday

Last night as Desiderio and I sat sharing our hot chocolate, I looked at him in a new almost-unbearably sweet light: my younger brother's friend.

They have been through death and almost wars together and now they don't quite know what to do. I have room to love them both forever. They are both such clear channels of divine love.

I'm very happy. Even knowing that I have to leave. I know by now that loving doesn't stop.

Tuesday
18 March

Ticket picking-up day.

Not ticket getting—but a Ganesh.

The Leaving

The leaving was a wrench, no way to prepare for the scream of feeling leaving an arm behind, no way to feel intact.

Desiderio took me on the speeding bullet (my name for his big motorbike) toward Pondicherry. We negotiated early evening traffic of lorries and buffalos, buses and cows, mopeds and cycles and general processions, toward the seaside town, through fishing villages, denser and denser masses of people, garishly painted buildings, cries for life, flowers, tea shops, bicycle repair, and spice merchants.

And the lights went out.

The city suddenly quiet, we found our way in the dim to our special travel agent in a cavernous French colonial mansion on the promenade at the sea. The Bay of Bengal.

The diminutive Mr. Patel sat at his big desk in a big dark room with a candle by his elbow.

Glasses slipped down his nose, he peered intensely at his huge book of plane schedules. Madras, Kuala Lumpur, Tokyo, LAX, Seattle, Vancouver. It was too dark; he couldn't see. The pronouncement came. "I can give you a ticket to LA and there will be a reservation for you for the rest of your journey—and that ticket will cost THIS MUCH."

And then he said, "Don't worry—you can't push nature. Mother and Sri Aurobindo will take care of everything." I paid him a wobbly great tall stack of rupees, made note of THAT MUCH money for the rest of my passage, and we walked out into the darker night straight to the temple shop and Desiderio carefully chose a small amethyst Ganesh for insurance.

The last days have been a torture of moments. I've been in a daze, newly orphaned by my father, deeply in love with where I was, who I was with, the pure joy of being beside my brother in this peanut field, the warmth of it all.

The warmth, though, was becoming heat. Melting. A deep relaxation seeped into the panic. The temperature rose above skin temperature. Lying on my bed, no covers, losing the sensation of the edges of my physical body, the breeze can enter my molecules, passing through me without impedance. I am fully part of the universe, mixed with bird-song and the scent of jasmine.

The day is closer.

Fear rises again. I cry. I stop stopping smoking, taking comfort in the pungent exotic beedies Desiderio has left in my house.

Waves of everything come over me as I pack my bags. Not all my things. I have agreed with myself to be an ingredient in the experiment of Auroville.

The last night we lay in his cool granite upper terrace room, the inner private place open to the night. Close, beyond physical passion. Held in a higher, brighter plane, drifting through each other's dreams.

We emerged in the dawn hand in hand to the waiting quiet gathering of new friends, new neighbours. Small gifts and talismans to take, a funny list of things to bring back: American underwear, good chocolate, bungee cords, French perfume, hair conditioner, something from the exalted Red Indians for D, comedy tapes for my brother.

I turn to the road, to the waiting car. My bags are stowed, embraces of farewell. The comforting presence of my brother to the airport. This time, the reverse four hours of suicidal Indian traffic, made with my almost-twin. So different going in this direction. When he was to catch me on landing, I was afraid of his goodness, his spirituality, his discipline. Now this boy, so happy to have his sister by his side, easily and innocently tempted to taking me shopping with promises of ice cream, would chauffeur me anywhere. I fed him and cared for him.

And now we have a plot. I will return to Canada, to give my mother what she needs—me—for a time, and John will stay behind as bait for her to come also.

Time crept and leapt; the airport loomed.

I'm ticketed, documented, and passed through the gate. But wait, I haven't said goodbye. I can see John standing, left behind, and I sweep aside the soldier blocking my way, machine gun diagonal across my path. I look in his eye, look up into his heart, and "Never mind that," I tell him, "I have to hold my brother one more time."

The plane rises. I sink pressed back in my seat, pulled back to the red soil of India and rising at the same moment. I am ripped. But on my way, surrendering and trying to turn toward the west, my mother, my son and sisters, beautiful island home floating at the extreme other edge of this Pacific Ocean.

21 March 87

Kuala Lumpur

Tokyo

LAX

Tokyo—great hot chocolate! Out the window I see:

Korean Air,

Iran Air,

Egypt Air,

United,

Air France

Air India, Japan Air,

KLM, and

Malaysian

This flight is so long. The flight attendants won't tell us how long or far. We compare our watches: counting forwards, tracing backwards, and give up.

I am vaguely concerned about the connection in LA and hold my Ganesh a little more tightly.

The landing at Kuala Lumpur is smooth, but my ears hurt. Many of us join in the airport lounge for gin.

One step closer—or further. The agonizing jump to Los Angeles.

Landing, my ears are more painful.

In the labyrinth of the airport, my terminal, luggage, and counter are found. There is no reservation. Worse, no actual flight even. And the last blow: if I could get a ticket, if there were a flight, it would cost forty-two more dollars than I have in the world.

Breathe. Don't faint.

What to do?

Find a shower, have some tea. A few dollars less at this point won't make much difference. But the longer I'm marooned here the worse it's going to get.

Black Saturday, my mother calls that day.

Phone home, they say. Have your mother wire the money. Several calls, collect. Verdict: one may not send money, by telephone, from the Gulf Islands, on a weekend. It's Saturday. Helpless anguish for my mother.

Sinking.

I breathe to the sky. Lift my eyes, a silent call. Help me now.

I have a sudden feeling, immediately, to turn. I whirl to the young man standing behind me and ridiculously pop out the question, "What high school did you go to?"

The one next to mine in Vancouver and ten years later. Clean, fresh, an angel looking for someone to rescue. "I will help you; I will get you a flight, I will give you the money. Don't worry."

He does. I am being carried by magic.

Exhausted almost to my end, the young man stayed by me and walked me to the next waiting airplane.

By now I am in searing pain, eardrums about to burst, knowing there are several more ups and downs to endure. I still need help.

A gang of rougher-looking angelic beings appear, filling the airplane row on either side of me. The old woman settled next to me folds me into her compassion.

To the end I will remember her hard-to-grasp statement: "My sons are barnstormers, we're on our way to Alaska, but"—pointing—"that man, that man will help you." That man looks like a gorilla, but I put myself in his hands. No choice. Two more plane changes, now that I have an actual ticket. I clearly can't do this alone.

Trust it. I am being carried home. The giant rugged man, fetching my baggage, organizing this moment of my life, is an experienced traveller, a forward for the Philadelphia Flyers. Big angels I'm getting.

I've lost all sense of destination. All thought gone, I am only being carried now, lost in pain of every kind.

Relief floods as Vancouver draws near. This part of the journey, nightmare mixed with blinding flashes of light, is done.

Home. A flesh-and-blood sister is at the airport. Six months. I've sailed away and flown back. She can have no idea of the grinding shifts that have taken place.

She seems to recognize me. I guess I must look sort of the same on the outside. She's missed me fiercely and doesn't yet know that she's going to have to keep on missing me.

The First Trip Back

I am trying to be—here—now—trying to land, pulling to have all the parts of me assemble in one place. She doesn't see that, my sister.

I'm glad.

My mind is reeling with responsibility, drawn to my mother, still another small sea journey away—tomorrow. Dizzy and unbalanced from it all, the sharp pain piercing my ears dulling finally to an ache, I am embraced by a dear friend who pulls up in her car before we've even taken my bags to the house. A warm hug and she pulls back, holding me at arm's length. Softly, she says, so no one else can hear, "You're not staying." Oh dear. I fall inside. I didn't want to come and say, "Hello, goodbye, your brother's gone, and Dad, and I'm leaving you forever too." Tears mist me again. She holds me close again and will not tell the secret she's seen.

There is joy too. The orphan feeling is passing with the weeks since the death of my father. He wasn't well, after all, for a long time. I am relieved for him, and somehow celebrate with him for finding the courage to make the leap. I know my mother will survive this nicely; she's more anxious for my arrival at this moment than bereft. I had felt her helplessness on the telephone, like a quicksand dream when she couldn't rescue me home.

Tomorrow I will be there.

One more thought is in my head. Persistent. I feel compelled to rush to the man who unknowingly inspired the spark, the mad possibility, that when I undertook this journey to the other side of earth I could go some other way than flying. I could step off the extreme edge of the West, literally, and sail beyond the horizon.

I want to run and thank him.

Arrangements are made to get me to the island.

There is a soft, quiet welcome from everyone I ever knew as I come from the ship directly to an open rolling meadow on the sea. In silence, a loving recognition, and our attentions turn to the circling eagle above, holding Karl's soul. We make our way to the beach and watch his ashes scattered on the sea.

I shout, inside, my thank-you to the sky. And silent thoughts to my father. The memorial I'd missed.

Wednesday
April

I'm becoming grounded, although I will never be the same again. Every beautiful thing I see, I seem to feel

through the eyes of Desiderio, or want to tell him, or send it
to him—everything.

Thursday

I feel I've been to the moon and back, or some other
planet, so clearly now do I see the earth as some small ball,
as if from a great distance. And also that I belong there. One
cannot make that sort of profound journey, even if it is all
inside, without it having some sort of impact. A shocking
slow reverberation of timeless catapult. I'm not sure even
if I look the same, although everyone who waited for my
reappearance on this side seems satisfied it's me and glad
of my presence.

I've left part of myself behind and may not feel complete
again until I can go back.

The forest here is a wild thing. Its rampage of growth is
only stopped by the edge of the sea. The evergreen trees are
all around, and tall, tangled through with the mad twists of
arbutus, smooth trunks gleaming red in morning rain. The
ocean today is a smooth gentle pink-blue the same as the
sky, differentiated only by the distant darker blue of islands
to the south.

Mom has made a fire against the cool, damp chill. I will
go in.

A letter from you has arrived.

How can I be eloquent enough to express that I know you are a companion of my soul, that you and I are right? You reflect me in a way that lets me learn—about me. You are showing me about peace and beyond the emotions I am familiar with, a place much wider than I dreamed.

The Mother and Sri Aurobindo are here too. Who do you think got me home in one piece?

I can't remember what I've actually told you and what I wanted to say.

Desiderio, ne me faites pas penser que je vais vous trouver sur le plancher quand je reviens. Je ne désire pas que tu tombes. Attendez jusqu'à ce que je suis près de toi.

I look for whales in the dark swirls off the point. When I feel them so strongly, searching the water each time I glance out, often they are there—or come in the next days.

Monday, Easter

Last night you came and were with me on a beautiful white cruise ship under a blue blue sky. You took my hand as we walked through the entire length of the ship and then climbed up to sit in the sun and fresh sea air.

I awoke still feeling the pressure of your hand in mine, and also where you had touched my foot, which made me smile.

Tuesday

Our weekend guests have left. A completely peaceful day. There is enough breeze to gently move the long stalks of orchids on the deck, only making me more aware of their presence, but the sea is completely silent—graceful soft drifting with no sound even at the shore.

Soon this utter peace will be broken by the constant summer stream of American yachts—but the holiday hum in the air means a season of work for us here on the island.

There are perhaps two to three weeks of our precious winter solitude remaining. Then the whole atmosphere will change in a rush. The population will triple at least.

But while we still consider it winter, before the strangers come, I am free to wander over the cliffs and through the forest, finding my way on deer trails. The ferns are unfurling and the evergreen trees are all sprouting soft fresh colour at the ends of their branches.

23 April 87

My thoughts of you are echoed by the deep quick pulse of a freighter passing by. I can't see it, but if I were to leave my sheltered spot on the beach and climb to the top of the knoll, I would know exactly where to look. But I won't because every ship I see only makes me want to be on board, coming back.

My summer will be pleasant. Filled with days of hard work and time for absolute leisure. Time to read and breathe, but underlying every moment—India.

An intense homesickness for Auroville persists. I try not to let my mother see the anguish. That I am crumbling. But then I sit with her and try to explain. To honour her non-clinging open-hearted motherhood that lets us be free, my sense of exploration and wonder at it all outweighing fear. And I urge her to leap also.

She will follow me back to the end of the earth to see for herself. I am proud of her bravery, and we find a new footing of truth, enjoying our roommate-ness. There are shared meals, moments, and comfort in having each other there as we each prepare ourselves for another chapter. Still there are waves of hurt, of miscomprehension, but manage-able mostly, and capped with excitement as my heart turns freely to the East.

I've come down the stairs straight from my bath to the beach, not bothering to dress. I'm only in my robe, which has been discarded, with my paper and pens and sunglasses and a clock (so that I can join Mom for lunch before I go to work at two). I did grab my bathing suit but have not put it on. No one is around or likely to be, and if they come it will be only someone else searching for a secluded place. And they will go away.

Living on the edges of places—islands, continents—pre-pares me to explore the edges of my mind and soul.

An old friend has a beautiful racing sloop; on days when he's not chartered, a favoured few, a willing crew, are rounded up.

Lying at full length in the cockpit, with my eyes closed, I feel the warm, clear sunlight from above and the cradle of the sea below. We are flying among the islands. I am watching, in my mind, through the hull of the boat, the water streaking by. The boat is flying. And then I am—high above the mast looking down. Brought back quickly, reluctantly, by a call to come about.

I am, before many seconds pass, caught in the delight of the day. Against the blue sky, the lines of the huge sails hesitate for a moment as the sloop swings around. I pull with all my might, winching it in, securing the sheets, settling in to enjoy our new tack—the edge of the sail in the water, rails in the water. The sea and the wind let us revel in their power. I feel my strength—feet braced, all of me braced, to hold the tiller. Crashes below as everything finds its natural level. I glance down in, laughing. Things are everywhere. Rolled off, down, into corners. With relief I see my camera safe.

I wish you were here.

We sail a little more sedately into our port, the crew, weather-beaten and by now cold and tired. We glide by several friends out in their smaller boats catching the little breezes in the shelter of the bay. Shirtless, sunning, chatting from boat to boat, we are hailed as we return from our adventure.

*****

Your letter welcomes me home.

The last few weeks have been difficult. The work I need, to earn enough to come back, is likely but not certain. My determination to leave here early in September doesn't waver, but it's been a constant test of patience and faith.

I planted the garden, cut back the wilderness a bit (ever trying to take over), read books, read more books. I kept remembering that my main purpose for being here now is to be with my mother, which never feels like a chore or an imposition. I would like to do more for her than I do, but she says she doesn't want to become dependant on me because I am leaving so soon. She is not, in any case, a dependant sort of woman.

I have been working sporadically until now, but have been given word yesterday that I am definitely on the yes list for the resort I wanted. They will be pulling a full staff together by June 15 and then will go full steam for July and August. It will be enough. What a relief.

So now I am on holidays. But really, I will have to make all arrangements soon because the rest of the summer will be completely non-stop.

Mom has gone to the city for a few days and the neighbours are away. I can walk anywhere and see no one. Absolutely alone. I've filled the house with honeysuckle for

its fragrance and the flamboyant blossoms of rhododen-
drons and brilliant poppies.

The sea out the window is a startling slice of blueberry
ripple ice cream. The sun is low in the sky and shining over
the gleam of the greens and the golden hills of wild broom.

It is nearly hot chocolate time here too.

I can feel you laughing at me all this way. No, I don't
have plans to measure myself drastically. I'm not going to
run all the way back, I will likely be able to fly. I've had my
ear re-examined and will see a specialist in the next weeks.
It will be fine.

I think an overland trek from London to Nepal would
certainly entail unimaginable tests.

The baby fawns are growing as fast as our summer
gardens. They are still very tiny, though, and spotted and
beautiful. Often on my way to work in the morning I stop
and watch them bounce from the road into the long grass
and trees and disappear. Work has definitely started and
will continue now as a marathon until the end of August.

We've been having a bit of a mail strike; I hope my letters
have reached you.

Arriving home from work I light a warming fire in the
hearth. The house is quiet—I can only hear the flames softly
crackling and the ceiling fan going round and the birds
outside. It's cold today. I'm tired and feel alone.

Pearl-grey sky and sea and some muted blue islands in the distance are the only things in sight past the glassed-in front of the house.

The just-past-full moon comes up orange over the ocean. Two more of her cycles to go.

At last, down finally to counting days, not months or weeks, until it's time to leave. I am probably more here than I have been so far. Occasionally I feel a somehow-not-unpleasant emotional wave about those I will leave behind here, but it seems now that it has always been inevitable.

My son, Ashley, is here with me and seems to be taking the whole thing comfortably in stride. He has grown so much since I saw him last. Soon he will be taller than I and his hands have changed from last year's exact duplication of mine to a longer-fingered version. His voice is changing. He is still green-eyed with the right one mostly brown. He is steadfastly refusing to be brainwashed that by going away I am deserting him. Good.

I enjoy the pleasant occupation of giving untransportable favourite things, mostly to my sisters. Mom insists, "Susan will be returning; just take care of them for her."

But there are no words for letting go of Ashley, not knowing when or how to see him next. My boy, becoming a man, understood my dream more clearly than anyone, felt the expansion of his own universe of possibilities. Taking my hands, a direct look and his words—"I'm proud of you"—then he's gone.

The turmoil I feel at leaving here is not as great as when I left India.

Gently the bonds are made more elastic. I don't know how much I will miss this place; it is so beautiful, and I was born here, and the leaving is not from a desire to get away but rather the responsibility to go forward.

I am on the ferry after a day in the city. The last trip with my car. It has been sold.

I've always relished the approach to the ferry terminal—driving through the busy city, over bridges, down the freeway, knowing that the traffic will thin out as people swing off onto exits along the way until fewer and fewer of us are left. Finally coming to the end, where there is no choice but to drive past the shore, along the narrow finger only two car lanes wide, a full mile straight out into the sea, and then off the end, onto the waiting boat.

We are going forward in a total blanketing fog. It is bright with light bouncing on all the little molecules of water in the air. No worry of being lost; we will simply pull into the dock on course. The captain knows exactly where we are.

Now we have entered the island group. It foils the fog and the luminous cloud is left behind. Here, inside, the bays and channels are clear, misty around the treetops—and calm.

Leaves are turning golden and red; the air is crisp in the mornings and at night. Time to leave.

Ten more days, then:

Vancouver

Seattle

London

Paris

London

Moscow

New Delhi

train to Madras.

Off to INJA!
New Delhi

I install myself in a little hotel for the day, leave my luggage, and throw myself out into the chaos to manifest a train ticket to Madras. I choose a rickshaw, or he picks me, and off we go.

The scene at the station is frantic. The man at the window says "No"; I can't have a ticket for the next train, I must reserve twenty-four hours in advance because I'm a foreigner. I tell him, "No," that won't work because someone is meeting me from THIS train.

The dashing young driver steps in, pulls me aside, and says "Come with me, I will manage this for you."

We pile back into the rickshaw, fly and jolt our way into narrower streets that become back alleys. I wonder over my sanity, my safety. We lurch to a halt in a little lane full of closet-sized shops.

He helps me descend, ushers me to a chair, and I'm offered a cold drink. It's his brother's travel agency. Having surrendered to a state of faith, I hand over a great pile of rupees and watch him go off to handle the matter. Here I am, marooned in an alley somewhere in New Delhi, my worldly possessions in a third-rate hotel somewhere else in the city. But I have a cold drink, and everyone is smiling.

He does return, triumphantly, with ticket in hand. He will take me back to my hotel to rest during the daytime hours and fetch me again in time for the train. Trusting his gracious honest concern, I am able to relax. I am his project for the day.

I give myself all the advice I can think of, mostly "Just don't be scared," and I'm off again. My faithful driver bounces us through the rush hour back to the train station. Chaos. Thousands and thousands of people. Once again, he takes the lead, takes my bags, and confidently forges through the crowds to my car. I am being treated like a lady. My bags are put on the train, and then I am helped in too.

I settle in.

I'm wondering how to go about finding some tea as a passenger asks out of the blue if I would like some. Ah!

Very quickly I find out that the trip will take twice as long as I was told. I am worried, geographical dyslexia kicking in fully.

Thirty-six hours of dozing, chatting, sharing food, more stories. Another passenger has a daughter in North America, and so feels duty bound to make sure that I am taken care of. His car and driver will meet the train. If Desiderio isn't there, they will take me to the Taj hotel.

He is there.

LIGHT GREEN NOTEBOOK: VELLAYAPPA AND SONS

Saturday 11:20 p.m.
17 October 1987

Hungry—check the tin for biscuits—check the biscuits for termites; we're having a war, them and me. Them and everyone. But I intend to make it a crusade. They have started to eat this beautiful house; it quickly becomes part of the daily routine to thwart their game.

It's turned hot again—the monsoon is also due—scorpion time.

Beaded Vest

Fascinated with the beadwork in an Auroville workshop, I take to wondering what a vest would look like if it were only beads.

I make a drawing and take it to another artist to have a painting made, and then a pattern is made from that. The design is an open lotus covering almost the entire back; the leaves will wrap around to the front of my body. There will be only one.

It is a thing of beauty. A solid supple layer of tiny iridescent beads. It has weight in my hand, and feels a bit like magical armour.

Double-threaded nylon thread, every bead twice threaded. Connections are double-knotted and then sealed with the heat of an incense stick. One lady x one month = 75,000 beads = $375.

Priceless.

19 October 1987

The typhoon missed us. Lightning in the distance, no sound of thunder. There isn't always, here, in any case. The humidity is high, too high. They say in about three weeks it will cool down, maybe enough to make it to the beach for a swim! Sleep in the afternoon is more than suggested. All bodies simply collapse during the worst of the day.

20 October

Thunder—no lighting. Rain in the night. The monsoon is trying to reach us. Not yet here. Not quite yet.

This morning, while cycling to Aspiration (what a wonderful name for the village), the air is thick with moisture.

Red road a mire from the rain, even going downhill felt like a slow heavy swim. Water hangs in the air, not falling, clouding my eyes. I've somehow accomplished all my destinations. I've managed arrangements, got things done, slept heavily, damply, in the afternoon.

My new photographer cohort came for tea. On Friday he will begin to show me the darkroom ropes. I'm interested in getting serious about this thing. He seems pleased that I want to be involved only with the pictures. No other work.

Accordingly, projects are being handed to me. Had I waited to return to Auroville, slipping in, in that regard, would have been harder.

Evening

Something quietly large and wide is going on here. It feels like a peacefulness that is new and somehow different, quiet. It feels like a state that is going to last for some time. I am not wanting, or expecting, missing, or waiting for anything.

The day passed so peacefully I lost the passage of it. It just was—or is.

Lost in each instant.

There is enough time to accomplish everything—or nothing. To be in the morning near you pruning the lemons and tangerine trees, to give you tea, to have the sweet soft rain come upon us.

21 October

Morning assignment: photographs at the school.

23 October 87

Letter to Mom

It feels like two weeks that I've been here. Although, thinking hard and looking at the calendar, I realize it's been a month now since landing with my entry visa. And almost before we can turn around, you will be here! Do you know the details yet, or even which way around the world you will come?

It's still pretty hot—too hot for the beach for me still—and the monsoon hasn't come. It's trying, though. It's night; the house is open. I am in only camisole and pants (silk from Paris) and am drenched. The humidity is so high that sweat doesn't seem to ever have a chance to evaporate.

In the darkroom today we took the cold water (the only kind) temperature—they say it's cooling: 29°C. Don't worry, by the time you get here it will be great and you will need a sweater at night. So many people besides me and John are looking forward to your arrival. You will have a lovely welcome.

Yes—the darkroom! After shooting a roll of black and white film this weekend, I will be initiated into tropical-style developing! So happy. There seem to be countless photographic projects and a real need for people interested in doing them. A few of us seem to be being ejected full steam into those activities and it looks quite possible that I will be able to do that only. Hooray!

My beaded vest was indeed finished and is beautiful. We calculated 75,000 beads! I will be doing a photography project in the Village...more soon.

love always, Susan

Saturday 24 (night)

We can talk sometime? Somehow when you really were far away it was easier. I felt you there. Did I imagine it, or wish it? I don't think so.

When I was there—away—if I wanted to talk to you in the day or before I went to sleep, I just could write and send it without worry of disturbing you. You just could pick it up and read it whenever you had a moment and then a reply would come, to my amazement and joy.

I won't send this. We will talk. Face to face.

Sunday

Woke to rain. Peaceful day.

Long teatime and happy light talk.

27 October 87

Worth it to stay home from the kitchen tonight to witness the crystals in my window do their slow fiery dance against the night sky.

An unexpected visitor is waiting by the bicycle house for Desiderio when I come home. I remember him from my visit last winter, but he obviously doesn't recognize me, and looks quite lost, confused by my arrival. He tells me that he can't see, hardly at all. An accident, he tells me as I invite him in for tea.

As we talk, Desiderio quietly arrives home and begins his daily practice of hatha yoga asanas. His rooftop terrace, sheltered in the garden canopy, is a perfectly private, elevated space that captures any soft evening hope of coolness as the sun stops baking the red earth. The heat dissipates— a little.

I deliver his friend, settle him in to wait in the evening half-light, then happily return home to spend a luxuriously quiet evening with my books. I am completely exhausted from cycling around Auroville all day, camera strapped on, freelancing my way to photographer-hood.

I am included in their dinner plans. We combine all our food and talk, and laugh at and with each other, and later walk him home.

Soft night—new moon and misty stars as we find our spot in the amphitheatre and sit closely. Out of the easy silence he says to me, "I didn't come here since you left."

I am home again after eternities. Safe and gathered in his arms, hardly knowing the tears fall. I am lost in remembering our parting. His steadfast reassurance as the car took me away that last morning. The six months, half a year of being on the other side of the world, now seem like one night's dream. The feeling of our being out among the stars somewhere, realizing it and not caring if we ever come back, or ever touch the earth again. When he asks for words, I tell him, and he holds me closer.

Friday
30 October 87

No worry here about taking rest if you need to, and don't do it voluntarily. You simply will be flattened by something.

We seem to have achieved monsoon status. It's cool enough to have closed most of my windows (but not the door). John reports having closed the flaps on his room. There's been a run on candles and matches. The current was out from last evening well into the morning today. A forewarning of the weeks to come. This year I feel the coolness immediately, although I KNOW it's not cold by any previous standards in my life. We are all mentally locating our winter sweaters, socks, jackets, shawls, and blankets for when the temperature will plunge in the next month or so. Perhaps hitting a low of anywhere from 19°C to 15°C is the most dramatic estimate.

Too tired to continue.

31 October 87

A difficult day. It helps somehow that it's not only hard for me, but for Desiderio also. We both came home early this morning from our outings, not wanting to face anything or anyone more, except that I do want to join John for dinner.

One of the truly nice things about being alone is a light-hearted freedom. I should remember that at times like now; I feel rootless, temporary, and wish I had someone to share my dreams with. I've even gone so far as to reminisce fondly about being married. Someone was there, someone to hold me. I remember also how often I didn't want that. And about this temporary sort of feeling, wanting to put down some roots—even to plant actual trees that I could watch grow, wanting to not HAVE to move again unless I want to. Why is that? What is it about? Why do I feel so EMOTIONAL today?

The air is heavy and unsettled. Trying to monsoon. It didn't rain again today. Changes, worrying, are in the air—waiting. Settle down. Also, it's Halloween—which I don't like.

Vision Note

While sitting quietly, a hand reached out from the stars, toward a light or a crystal, closed on a golden ring. The hand opened, releasing the ring, which turned slowly away, still turning up and off into space. Vivid colour.

Sunday
1 November 87

Dream notes

I was at a gathering with many people. Looking down, I discovered, to my great interest, that my skin was coming off. No blood, no pain, but a thick, hard layer, like a shell, about a quarter-inch thick over my entire body. I could look underneath and see the new surface—tender, a little red from being unexposed—but knew it would be all right. I wanted to get away so that I could take off the old layer. I remember thinking in the dream that the layer was so thick I would actually appear thinner.

The night before: I only remember being out on the ocean, either with a very small boat or none at all, being passed very close by what looked like a war barge to me. Danger of swamping. The person I was with was afraid.

1 November (day)

I have planted some cactus cuttings in front of my house that Desiderio gave me yesterday. Also branches from a lovely tree he handed me as he was pruning. After they root I can plant them wherever I want, he said.

Did he pick up what I was thinking yesterday? I think so.

What else does he know? This morning when I went to take the curd, he was waiting with tea for me (and a chocolate bar) beside his chair. I told him I had spent the afternoon with a girlfriend. He sighed and smiled with obvious relief, saying, "I wondered—it must be very strong—all afternoon I was picking up images of you—and you and her—and you."

I told him my dreams, and he smiled again and said, "That's good—it's good," and kissed me, and said, "It will go on for a long time, you know." We talked about how to keep quiet through it all, and somehow carry on with the daily "outside" work we have to do, and all those nights of work in dreams.

I've spent the day cleaning my house, and have seen no one else. It crossed my mind to invite neighbours for lunch, but I was too content in my Sunday ritual: washing, polishing with Mansion polish, fresh flowers everywhere, cushions out in the sun for the morning, laundry, finished my book. Tonight I will start reading Sri Aurobindo's diary.

Forgot one thing. Lately, a sort of visions have been happening. Noting just for interest of progression and to maybe discover some meaning.

2 November 87

Today my world is slower and more manageable. The photographer came this morning at 9:30. We talked for a while. I told him about wanting more time to "land" and then start again from a stronger footing. He just smiled and said, "Of course you do." Almost by that declaration I had passed some test. A first step. Most of the day was spent happily in the darkroom. The contents of the film was almost incidental, getting the process learned. As a side effect, we are, amusingly, absorbing some Italian.

Desiderio passed by after his work. Do I want to share his dinner? Of course.

He had been thinking, he said, after we had eaten, after, in the midst of a monsoon rain, discussing the world's water problem (is it possible to make more water? More hydrogen and oxygen?), that I might like to cycle to the beach with him after work tomorrow, if it isn't raining. It almost doesn't matter, he was thinking of it. Of me—and him. I could hear his heart beating as he came and held me before I left.

We both will attempt an easy dream night.

4 November 87

I should have been able to say that I only came to see if you felt like going for a walk, with no drama—as you would be able to say with almost anyone there. But your other woman friend still throws me off balance by so strongly not acknowledging my presence. I'm sorry.

5 November 87

Full moon day

After a rainy trip to Pondy, soaked to the skin, eating ice cream, laughing as the waiter continued hopelessly to mop up the puddles of water we were making as we sat with our chocolate treats, hot sweet coffee, and tea. Beedies with endless piles of matches, which are part of the smoking ritual in the monsoon, poring over his magical photos of flowers. Gentle, delicate. Stunning colours. Each one caught in his way, with no depth of field—hardly at all—their vividness suspended.

The rain stopped. Back on the street the people have emerged into the fresh clear after-storm light. In our splashes of primary colours, uniformly drenched, no longer dripping, we don't look wet anymore.

Through the instantly flooded streets, steaming villages, herds of soggy goats, we raced cosily home, he wrapped in a shawl, me enveloped in the flying ends of it, behind him on the motorcycle.

Noon. Home, into dry clothes, hot tea into me. The loot of fruit and vegetables, henna, incense, jasmine from the city put safely away. Feet up. Soft breeze. Drowsy, sleep now for a while.

*****

Towards oneness: isn't active sharing—of views, work, material things, feelings of the purest loving we can feel— somehow acceleration for all of us, our progression? Even in our own selves, whose edges merge—if we have edges— with everything else, each instant of peace or joy (how can even they be separated?) will pass on and on and on, as will each frustration or angry thought.

Desiderio came to have his photograph taken. He sat and let me do it, looking straight into me. Shaking, I hoped not too much, I pushed the shutter button again and again.

Contemplation—The Importance of Art

By externalizing our vision and merging views of all different possible perspectives, because the awareness of each of us is coloured and shaped by our reaction to seeing the universe from our particular point of immersion in it, we can only help increase our awareness—our understanding— our progression.

Even by looking at a painting or photograph, or touching something that some other hand made, we react in turn to the joy and love and even struggle with which it was brought into the physical open. It is an important ingredient, an acceleration in the uplifting of the whole.

6 November 87

The relieved sleep after the full moon. Fresh start. Things will be accomplished, revealed, at their own pace.

6:45 p.m.

Flowers becoming real, clear, like a veil dripping away in front. I could move around. Single blue blossoms of the tree of life. Some of the flowers photographed this morning. Suddenly a woman's eye, then the other one behind the flower. The eyes were alive, moving, looking at me. The Mother, I felt, I feel, just making her presence known.

*****

I think this climate helps to experience feelings such as this. Where it's warm enough. Warmer than your body. To lie down at night, in the total darkness with no covering to help identify (by its very presence) the perceived boundaries of your body, and to feel the weight of the universe not only from above but as if in suspension, cushioned in a crystal ball. Scent of flowers never stopping, there each moment. And the sound of it all: always birds, orchestras of frogs, punctuated by music, jackals, wind in the trees. Any possible lull filled by constant cricket chirping. Every speck of every concept is so full—but not too full. Sleep will come quickly and it will all go on. And when I wake it will all be there, only the birds will be different and the sun will be thinking about coming in my windows. Or it will be raining.

Saturday a.m.

It was—of course—doing both.

To Pondy with a girlfriend, in the taxi!

Home by a lightless motor rickshaw, and adventures and dinner in between.

Sunday
10 November (morning again)

Back for a month. Already!

At dinner with Desiderio: "I was thinking to cut back the flowers in the shower."

Susan: "I was also thinking the same thing today."

Desiderio: "I know, you left a thought behind on the plant."

More photos of him today to replace my darkroom disaster Friday. He sat easily for me in the cactus garden, making fun, making faces, sitting quietly and letting me watch him in the light, light rain. As I knelt there, close in front of him, he opened his eyes, his whole self, and let me look inside. Without reaching, he drew me to him and held me very closely—for a long time.

A direct experience of oneness.

Monday

Success in the darkroom! I was nervous as I waited to take the film from the canister. The whole thing was very much like giving birth: sweating hot, having to go patiently through all the stages. Waiting, waiting. As each moment ticked by, knowing that the last attempt had been a completely mysterious failure, I checked every detail possible and chose to take the risk again.

We glanced at it only long enough to see that it "had all its fingers and toes" before rushing (slowly) to the drying cupboard. Tomorrow we will see what it looks like.

I bicycled home the four kilometres drained to exhaustion—and pleased.

8:00 p.m.

Too tired to tell you much more. I have been getting plants, pruning the vines over the shower, gathering laundry. No rest in the afternoon. I don't think it's too early for bed.

11 November

Is it too monsoony for this pen?

14 November

Questions for the morning.

Do you want me to live in the new addition to the house when your mother isn't here?

Why, if it isn't important, have you told me more than once that you feel like punching my brother?

Can I see your plans for the house—just to see? Those things would be nice for her; I don't need them. Do you want dinner?

Yes, I would love to create a home or help create a home for me. I kind of need that. If I had the money I would say yes. If this can be my home when she isn't here, let's do it. Make a corner where I can go and no one can see me if I don't want them to.

And I do love the nearness of you—the way we are. Sometimes I would like to have you hold me for hours. Just that. And I know that can be there, but not now. Just sometimes. And I can live without that part even, because I do.

16 November 87

Dream

Walking down a narrow path, tall grass, naked, going somewhere. Approached by a single-file line of old, thin village men going in the opposite direction. A little bit afraid. I didn't know if they were a threat to me.

I thought quickly, just maintain my purpose and carry on. I crossed my arms in front of my body, sort of hands-to-my-shoulders, knowing that none of me was really covered but making an attitude not to interfere with me.

We were going to collide if we all just kept going. They also were naked. I wondered what side of the path, in this country, do you pass on when walking? There was barely room, in any case, and I moved over to the right side and looked directly into their faces as we passed each other.

*****

Dawn—my birthday

Today of all days, the fairytale mushrooms that blossom on the anthills, making them enchanted castles, were waiting for me when I stepped outside. Once a year they come, for only a day! They are a gift to see; they catch your breath and make you stop.

Straight away I came back and loaded my camera with very fast film to catch them in the dawn light. Close, close, close, I crept. Little snails in heaven munching on their tender caps. The rising sun revealing the magic. Sweet gift of the night god's present of scattered Transformation flowers all around.

Desiderio has made me a painting. He burgled it into my house while sending me off into the garden in the opposite direction. It seems to me that there are crystals, inside each other, somehow connected to the whole of the universe.

17 November 87

Sometime, when you are not too tired and time is not pressing, can we talk? Because I am clumsy I am afraid that I may say or do things that you can misinterpret. I want everything to be clear and right between us. And I want to say the things to you, with you here, slowly and quietly, so that you can tell me if you don't understand, or if it is wrong.

I guess what I wanted to tell you was really very many things.

Remember the day you had a vision of a friend and I together, and we were? There was another thing that you saw and I didn't tell you. In the morning, when we both had come home in the midst of a difficult day, I had somehow been overcome by a feeling of temporary-ness and a sense of being unanchored, a transplanted-but-with-no-roots sort of feeling; I even went so far as to write down that I wished I could be, needed to be, somewhere long enough to plant something and watch it grow. To care not for a house because I live there, but for a home.

I had been trying to leave that completely out of my mind partly because I am relieved and grateful that you have allowed me to be here, and because January is a long way— another lifetime, and you or I or both of us may not remain comfortable with this proximity—and above all I don't ever want you to be uncomfortable or crowded. But the plants might live. Some of them look like they may take root.

Another thing was a longing to have someone to share my dreams with, and theirs. Not a possession or attachment but somehow to know without judgement—just to Know. The human comfort of that during this awkward struggle. Not always getting it right, but trying.

And then you had the strength in yourself and trust in me to be able to share those things in you, with me. No one could ever expect that from another. And given that, there are no possible expectations beyond.

One more: when you take my hand, or keep me in your arms, I find it impossible to worry or even to tell where I end and you begin—if we do at all. Only sometimes, and it is a quiet thing, I would like to stay close to you for a long time—just to be. I don't think that it's wrong, but I would leave very quickly if you ever tell me that you are going into your cave because of me.

Wednesday (for sure)
18 November 87

No need to deliver the last, just yet. A quiet, accepting understanding was just there this morning as I was greeted with a kiss, an offer of breakfast, and a making of tea for me too.

Daily stuff

Wake to the sunrise—just before—my first tea sitting on the window ledge as the clouds around the edge of the sky turn pink, then down the path in the garden to the toilet, 6:30 a.m., silk robe more than is necessary (it's very warm already), but one must wear something. Gathering my fresh flowers for the day on the way back: brilliant white fragrant Transformation blossoms that have fallen like Christmas snow in the night. All over India at this time of year, in the mornings, like the jasmine, they are ritually picked up and fill houses, are braided into long shining black braids, decorate cars and bicycles, and are generally carried around.

Off in the opposite direction through the garden to the shower. To breakfast with Desiderio. Shall we read the Sherlock Holmes novel, or not? The agave cactus is going to bloom; I must photograph it. We dragged out his airplane maps of the world (with France, of course, as the centre) to discuss exactly where in North America things are: he had no conception at all. We need a new map. Who next will grab the Dalai Lama book? One of us at least must get to the library.

The milkman on his bicycle is all dressed up and will be, I suppose, for the next month. We are at the beginning of a festival. They eat only after sundown each day, wear beautiful blue *lungis* and scarves, foreheads marked with white stripes and gold and orange, and go each night to the temple and sing. We will vaguely be able to hear them. Lovely as the singing and music and jungle drums are, by the end of the month we will all be a little frayed and almost ready to plot revenge.

Ten o'clock appointment in the darkroom. A sweat-making, blood-moving, breath-taking half-hour-almost ride. But it takes me, and makes me feel like singing, and totally makes pointless the morning shower.

How long do grasshoppers live? One has been in here for about three days and doesn't want to go out. He's very beautiful, a great big thing, and kind of hangs around close to me. Maybe he can be a pet—except that he's very noisy, crashing around. Not now—he's creeping up on something. But if he falls off the lamp and scares himself, or if I touch him softly and he jumps to the ceiling, he makes a startling noise like throwing a pencil. But I'm getting used to him and he feeds himself.

Before I could make my getaway from home, while I was still boiling the milk and rounding up cameras and thinking about dressing, I was absconded with to take an emergency

group photo. Twenty-five North Indians, here for an envi-
ronmental conservation conference, were leaving at noon.
"It only will take five minutes plus travelling time," so we
cycled off to the village of Kottakuppam (exactly, of course,
in the opposite direction from the darkroom). They were
very sweet and lined up eagerly in front of the camera. One
of the men came to me, his camera in hand. "A mystery," he
said, "it won't take a picture when you press this button."
I think that's what he said. You get so used to talking in
different languages on each side of a conversation. I took
it from him, was surrounded by a dozen serious-hopeful
faces, looked through the viewfinder, pressed a button. Sure
enough, nothing. I looked a little more closely, focussed
on the words ON-OFF- VOLUME. Volume?! I dissolved in
helpless laughter; shaking my head, I managed only to say,
"Of course this won't take pictures, it's a RADIO!"

Oh dear, this place is completely too much. On my way
again. But I was presented first with a handwoven rainbow
belt from their workshop, for service above and beyond the
call of duty. I ceremoniously flung off the one I was wearing
and put it on in front of the Tamil ladies who make them.

The darkroom: anxious to see my film. Today no water in
the cooler, water in the tap still too warm by 10°C. We need
a fridge in there—and have been promised a fridge in there.

The rest of the morning was spent with disaster stories
of jungle photojournalism. Shall we send my flower slides

to Bombay or Madras to be copied? Wading through the *tamas* in the air.

Jolly lunch with new cohorts. Frivolous happy talk from the controversial international characters crowded round our table.

Back on my cycle, under the feverish two o'clock sun, headed toward home. Halfway, I made a stop for photo-taking in the reafforestation nursery. Then close by in the deep red canyon and from the roof of a home overlooking it all. Tea in the construction shack with Desiderio. At four-thirty we raced each other home. Not top speed, but a push.

I stopped to check the mail on the way: no cigar.

Before the sweat stopped running, I mixed it with deli-cious cool water from the shower. Rivers of red dust from the canyon, a little blood from mullus (thorns) encountered in my climb, shampoo, sweet soap, cool water running clean. Fresh lungi, feet up, chai, book, quiet. Small sleep. Request from Desiderio to join him later in his night watch at Matrimandir—if I am awake. "Of course." And I set my alarm for nine-thirty in case I'm not. No moon, stars bright, no torch, I walk with the waited-for chocolate.

Did I want to tell him the things I had said I wanted to? "No," I said, "no!" He said, "No—not now. Then I will tell YOU some things," and I held my breath and asked if I should be nervous—no. We both said all the things under the dear Matrimandir, under the falling stars, with no moon. We walked hand in hand home, in the dark, both knowing the way, to where I will stay—there beside each other in the garden.

28 November 87

Bay of Bengal: late afternoon peacefully lying here. Nice breeze—not too hot. Only a few of us on this stretch between villages. Did you ever see or even imagine the possibility of a water buffalo bodysurfing? A herd of them has just been driven into the sea for a bath. They seem happy. The world is getting to be a stranger and more exotic place than ever I could have dreamed.

And now, even looking out to sea is different—isn't it? To know that it goes on and on—and to have been there. We come here in the evening sometimes, and swim, and wait for the sun to go down and the stars to come out. And often then I think of you.

11:00 p.m.

Curd making—no starter.

I hope that this doesn't entirely ruin your day, and mine too, incidentally.

I've made a mistake that will affect us both; I don't even think I should come in.

I hate it when I let you down, and it's such a basic thing.

*****

New noises that are part of daily life, some of which require an active response: candle going out noises, milk coming to a boil sound, bicycle coming home sound, geckos sound like little birds. Some birds sound like a tap dripping. The roar of the sea from way up the hill means it's probably too strong to swim. The plonk drip of the water filter, filtering. Head tilting, ear opening—whose motorcycle is that? Nighttime owls and jackals madness. Swish of bat wings, and the sleep-crowding village singing noises, that fold you in—hold you in—and mean to.

Monday morning
Last in November

This week:

    Photos in nursery (hibiscus)

    Bicycle to the beach

    Study French

6 December 87

The dream: I had trouble holding back tears when I awoke, until I realized that I must remain quiet and still and not stay caught in the emotion of it.

I was walking over soft rolling hills, looking down over farmland and country houses, roads, water in the distance, old acquaintances, and seeing with sadness that I didn't belong anymore. Worse, that I thought I had fit there and an overwhelming realization that I didn't, and would have to go—again—alone.

Crossing great distances, I spoke with my mentor to tell her I was moving on, to a new and strange (to us both) part of the world. It was a tropical place. Houses bright in the sun. A city. I would somehow have to make a place for myself there. We were on a hillside. People were around but with their backs to me. Strength and endurance were called for.

7 December 87

Last night after dinner it seemed appropriate to tell him the dream. We talked about what not making it—what not enduring—would mean. Also that I would make it.

Also that sometimes it would be easier, or comforting, or I would just like, to be simply held—for hours. And that perhaps not being held is part of it too, part of the whole thing—and important. To find the strength and quietness inside.

The rain stopped and we went for a conspiratorially happy walk. Bravely leaving behind shoes, torches, umbrella, warmly hand in hand under the racing clouds of a monsooned-out full moon night.

8 December 87

When I receive my next shocking piece of news, I will try to wait before I talk to you so that you are not subjected to any unnecessary drama. On the other hand, it is tremendously calming for me to have you laugh at me at those times.

*****

Today I received word from my mother that the money from you is not in the bank. Her letter took a month to reach me. She writes that you say it IS there, but...

My first reaction was shock, tears, sickness, panic, confusion.

If it is true—it isn't there and won't be—then I am irrevocably here, in India. On the other side of the world. You know that that money (of mine, which you owe me) was to keep me for the first year and to ensure the possibility of a return to Canada.

Now I am sitting in the midst of the monsoon in the middle of this garden, which still manages to be beautiful, assimilating the realization that no matter if I get homesick, no matter how badly I want to send for Ashley, those things simply are not possible.

For two or three months, likely one or two by the time you get this, I can survive. I am not placing my fate upon your shoulders for I chose to trust you. I can hardly bear to ask you once more—but I must.

Please.

Susan

10 December 87

La ligne des vêtements a tombe encore. Quelques tes choses sont sur la terre, et je pense qu'il peux pleut encore.

11 December 87

I'm not always very good at this unconditional love. I sometimes resent being allowed to be so close to you, even physically close, to never have you reject the knowledge that I love you completely.

You say that I should feel compassionate and gentle toward the woman who is still so obsessed by you. But for all I know you treat her the same way as you do me. Then no wonder she is seeming completely unreasonable in her attachment and jealous insecurity. Maybe I would be too.

Perhaps this yoga is a convenience. It's stopping short of becoming actual lovers.

You confuse my senses; where is the line? Is taking my hand, or holding me, or kissing my neck, all right and being any closer not? Those things seem natural and right and the closeness of you in no way feels against what I feel. And I do not want it to stop. But is it any wonder that sometimes I don't want to let go of you and then I find myself reacting in a quite human way of feeling resentment? Perhaps I should be entirely alone?

Most days, and even most of the hours of the remaining days, I feel only delight and calm and very much love for you. The other few moments are spent overcoming a more vital need to want to be enveloped by you, to have you want to keep me with you. I am fighting it. It wouldn't be much of a worthwhile battle if it weren't so strong. There is no need, I think, for us both to go into our caves.

*****

We are none of us children here (except, of course, the young ones born or brought here). Drawn to this curious place from every imaginable corner of the earth to struggle out our days, our nights, our dreams. Apart from the world but tied with the tendrils of our non-accidents of birth and relations, this place is a pinnacle trying to thrust itself through enveloping clouds to the shining unbounded wholeness of the universe. When we break through—slowly, slowly—this small planet will be forced to follow. The spreading growing roots of us will simply spring up all around, enmeshing the fabric of the world, strengthening, and pull us all together—up.

The fact of being here is often curious, startling, like the bloom of an evening primrose. As nighttime falls, cooling, all growth and flowering appearing finished for the day, but unexpected and unpredictable bursts of colour, fragrance (seeming to falter at first), and braveness of spirit blossoms in the night. It leaves us to wonder at boundless possibilities softly reflecting the caught moonlight into our watching eyes.

Saturday

As you foresaw, the shock period has hit. Recognizing the panic feeling triggered a memory of your words.

The shocking news this week that I must let go of the hope of the money owed to me being repaid. Ever. Don't react, just know it to better understand how I feel.

What is going on now, I think, is simply the impact of the last year. Nothing has changed in direction; rationally I believe still that I am right to have chosen to be part of the experiment that is Auroville.

To be here on an entry visa was a different feeling, as I suspected it would be, and took adjusting to. The possibility of really staying here, maybe forever, if I chose. And then the unsettling un-knowing of a home. That also has been quietly alleviated, with no move necessary. I told you—roots are down, my little plants are growing madly. Before many months they will even need pruning.

Now this latest bombshell has unleashed all sorts of repercussions. I know I am still alive and will remain so for a long time, I know I have a home and that I am loved, even on the other side of the world, but I feel panic, loneliness, fear.

The ability to stay or go by simply deciding, under my own resources, is suddenly gone. I know that I no longer quite fit there, and have no immediate desire to return. I guess I just have to remember that, and that the important thing was only to get here.

I won't post this for a few days, because you would worry too much to receive a letter from me ending (and beginning) on such a note.

Sunday

Don't worry. I think the panic has passed—for now. I talked to myself for a long time, and then to Desiderio. Some of those things that I was worrying about are so hard to say, or begin to talk about, but he always makes it easy for me. We both are struggling.

*****

Today, leafing through a book in the library, I came across a photo of Desiderio as a young man. Impossibly attractive; now, possibly fifteen years later, with the added ravages of all this time in India, he is devastating.

16 December 87

I sent a reply to the announcement that money isn't coming. I started other letters but have nothing to say. Stopped.

To my sisters

It made me sad to leave with everyone in tears and I've been dreaming of you. I don't know how you are. Will you ever come to visit us? It looks now like both John and I are stuck on this side of the world. Not stuck in not wanting to be here, because we do, but all of a sudden finding out that I have no money takes away the possibility of whimsically visiting Canada.

It's an adjustment, to be sure, but I am coming to grips with it. We may as well face the fact that I now also actually do live in India. How does that strike you?

I also have to trade missing my sisters for having John. I hope that you two derive the same quiet comfort from each other that we do. Delight is the key to life, he says.

We feel confident that Mom will join the ranks of mothers who come with some regularity, and it's nice. Everyone looks forward to someone's family coming and is glad for them, and for the family. It seems to make it easier for them in their far-flung corners of the earth to have been here, and seen and felt this place.

I don't want you two to be lonely for us. I want your lives to be happy. I think of you both when I watch the plants in my garden grow. Some I even transplanted (because it was only you who could grow things). But now I really needed to have the roots go down and leaves to sprout out. And they are.

Life here will not be easy, but a struggle in a different way from there. Each day there are undreamt-of obstacles, the largest and most obvious being India herself. But the joy of success in such a place is immeasurable.

I'm sorry if this doesn't reach you before Christmas; there are no prodding reminders of it here. No reminders at all. I don't even have a calendar. And I keep waiting to get cold: nothing.

We are conspiring to give John a haircut. I think it amuses him to be taken in hand by a sister. I have taken a photo of him that caused me to burst out laughing as I looked through the viewfinder. It was so John. We have dubbed it "Colonel John." The colonial in the tropics. Perfect. I will get into the darkroom and make copies for you.

Apart from the evenings that I have dinner with John or Desiderio (I cook for John, Desiderio cooks for me) I mostly get to be a hermit.

I think most of us here are voracious readers, relentless journal keepers, and early sleepers. We grab books from each other until the entire neighbourhood has read them. The library only physically checks out non-fiction, so novels can and do rotate endlessly. Much more sensible than each of us having to make the trip.

Each day, except for the rare one when we lose each other, I see John at some point, even if only to cycle past Matrimandir and wave at him on top and check to see if we have any mail!

Every morning I have breakfast or at least tea with Desiderio at about seven until we have finally to go to work (?!), me freelance photoing, him building that beautiful house still. Today he had saved a baby papaya for me. Not often are they small enough for one person to eat all at once. And he succumbed to letting me cut his hair in the garden. A major triumph of trust.

Tomorrow we have the final gathering together and choose the photos we have taken for Auroville International. They will be sent to America, the UK, France, Italy, Holland, Germany, Brazil, and Canada. A nervous day. Then I can get on with the other projects I've been asked to do a little more peacefully and quietly. Hopefully one by one.

I have to squeeze in three meetings and a date for tea in the afternoon. A friend is baking a cake. That's a major achievement; I don't dare miss it.

This morning even the flower I thought would remain a dead stick forever is vigorously sprouting green.

At 10:15 a.m. I'm sitting in a breezy open dining room, having been automatically supplied tea, as I wait for my third arranged meeting of the day.

I hope Mom brings her #22 sunscreen; I plan to abscond with it. Desiderio's last words this morning: "Watch your nose!"

I have cycled half of my ten kilometres today, which means, of course, that now before lunch is the uphill half. Oh, I will be fit at forty.

John says, when I ask if the postman has brought us anything, "No, hardly ever, you are here." I had said (laughing) that I would tell that one to you.

I feel concern for you both—in dreams and waking. Please write and tell me how you really are. Not knowing is not restful.

With love,

your Akka

Susan

Photography to do list:

1. Village Action

2. Health Centre

3. Village Schools

4. Environment

5. Employment and Training

6. Last School

7. New Creation

8. Isai Ambalam (Place of Harmony)

9. Ilaingnarkal (Nursery)

10. Promesse, Tindivanam Road

11. Village Evening Schools

12. "Get to Know You" Trip to Edayanchavadi

*****

Maybe the Mother brought me here, without even talking to me about it, and is now trying to see if I will break. There had better be a good reason, or is it a good enough purpose even for my own—my own what?

Why do I choose do life the hard way?

*****

Needless worry. Go smiling into tomorrow. Why should I have tears and hurt feelings when all of a sudden your other friend wants things to be easy, and I am expected to be glad. I am glad, if it's true, it's just that I had somehow allowed myself to feel awkward and hurt by her rebuff and, not wanting to cause you to have to make any sort of choice between our friendships, tried not to cause any drama.

But to hold hurt feelings and think up doubts of love is a choice.

I choose to let those feelings go. They both smiled at me. We all tried, with success, to make it through the afternoon. Desiderio was wearing, after seeing me dressed in the morning, the same colours in the same way—exactly. When done in that conscious way I take it as a statement of solidarity. When, as almost daily it happens, just happens, it is happy evidence of a bond. Sleep well—securely.

Even be content that we are hermits enough to have time to sort these things out.

23 December 87

Essay topics

"The Romance of Celibacy"

or

"A Never-Ending Courtship with the Divine"

"A Woman Alone in India for the Rest of her Life"

"Overcoming *Tamas* in the Tropics"

"Western Ways Won't Work"

24 December 87

How will we remember this day and the ones that will follow?

What reports will reach the West, frightening the families of all who are here—and Mom, coming in a week?

Last night, MGR, the First Minister of Tamil Nadu, died. BBC reports complete breakdown of law and order in Madras: rioting, looting. Twelve people there have been killed by the police.

The air is heavy with it, thick with it.

25 December 87

This is about loving and not taking it personally, about being here, and the Mother having some greater purpose.

You are not the object of my love. You are there and I do love you. But it's like a light shining around both of us— not just us, but you have been placed close to me for some reason, and the light shines love on me around and through, and on and through you. If I were to choose to become attached to you as the final, total focus of emotion (an easy thing to do because of the strength of human feeling and wanting a concrete safety), then I would be missing a greater and far wider thing.

28 December 87

Time in the garden; ideas are also germinating.

Simple silk kimonos

Panels of flowers, geometric designs for screens

30 December 87

The design of my garden worktable is underway. New concrete projects of photos are started.

Saturday trip to Mahabalipuram to catch, on film, Auroville planting trees outside Auroville. Also a visit to the crocodile and snake farms.

Tomorrow, Pondy shopping.

Monday Mom will arrive.

My new dinner combination: boiled potatoes, onions, mixed with wheat sprouts, chopped apple, masala, butter, and salt. Wonderful. Dessert: curd with cinnamon, peanut butter, and a little sugar. Equally a treat.

The milk is on for its second boiling of the day, and it's Wednesday evening tea at Matrimandir with Desiderio. The moon is about half full. Tired today.

Why, when on the last mouthful of my dinner, absorbed in my book, candle on the desk and a shawl warmly around my shoulders, was I suddenly invaded by a vision of myself sitting alone at my table in my little house on Pender Island—with a stabbing emotional pain and realization of aloneness past and to come? A flood of knowing.

Later

Maybe it's this freelance kind of work that allows me to move freely, and also makes any sense of security difficult. No one expects me anywhere daily or even regularly. Sporadically, yes: meetings and appointments.

31 December 87

Parce que demain est une nouvelle année, j'avais voulu que tu serais le dernier que je verrai aujourd'hui et demain—le premier. Alors, quand tu me taquine, j'été trop sensible et je ne pu pas demande.

Si n'est pas trop—je le veux.

New Year's day: a very early morning bonfire and breakfast, then start files at Matrimandir for archives.

3 January 88

If you say to someone who loves you, in that tone of voice, "I've had a gift of perfume," they just might be a little jealous.

Monday

Now it's my turn to be outside the wire mesh fence waiting, this time beside my brother, searching the faces streaming out of the Madras airport. He spots her and calls out. I watch her as she half-recognizes his voice with his Indian English accent and then her face lights as she finds us.

She's here.

It's all very heroic-seeming.

Her first journey truly abroad—Vancouver, London, Bombay, Madras—negotiated all by herself. Not so surprising, really, she is our mother, after all, but still, bravo. Her own adventure. Stories of "her" rickshaw driver in Bombay, the colours and sounds. Heat. Fatigue. And another four-hour taxi ride through the night.

We install her into the comfortable tropical-style socialness of the Guest House, with other mothers and families and travellers on their own, like I was.

And now, for the first time in thirteen years, to be with her only son.

There's a little awkwardness at first. They are each more easy with me. I step out of the way to let them find their way. They do. And then there's the round of invitations: to tea, to lunch, to dinner. Sightseeing.

How much to show or shield?

She's come only for us, her two first-born. She needs to see where we live. How we are. If we eat breakfast.

Our work makes it easy to visit and spend time during the day. We've started the video project at Matrimandir. What an interesting process. There are a handful of photographers. Film has been doled out and we have our instructions. The plot. For each shot that we take, there will be three views: telephoto, closer, and close up. The whole will be blended to a graceful melting of images.

I'm high up on the scaffolding in the late morning sun. I lean out as far as I can without falling to capture the geometry of machinery and men far below. Slightly dizzy-making.

Lunchtime.

I cycle home the three or four minutes through a shady forest path. And dive for my bed. Rest.

I wake and cannot lift my head from the pillow.

The fever has me. So fast.

It worsens.

I'm worried that Mom will be worried. She is.

This is not what I meant about giving them space to be together, but they are united in their caring for me. They have a mission, a purpose to the days.

Bone-breaking sweating pain I can't support anymore. I wobble to Desiderio in the night. I want to be held; I can't bear to be touched. He keeps me by him with the words, "We will call a taxi in the morning and take you to Pondicherry—your brother will come on his motorbike." In my blurred fog I realize that one of us won't be coming back right away. And it's me.

BLACK NOTEBOOK (1988-1990)

How sweet to think of giving me a notebook.

Chapter 1
Jan 88

Dr. Datta's Nursing Home

> I have nothing to read. I've made an explor-
> atory attempt down the hall to check for
> balconies and escape route stairs —and was
> brought back to my room, incarcerated with
> Dengue fever. A stringy black cat casually
> hurled himself across rooftops to the Blue
> Dragon Chinese Restaurant.

Instructions from the Doctor with stick drawings
of exercises

1. lying flat, raised knees—raise back

2. curling up (on back)

3. lying on stomach, opposite hand and leg to be raised alternately

4. raise both feet, toes and ankles flexed

5. Walking, stomach in, pelvic tilt

6. Hands over head walking

7. Deep knee bends out from wall, arms extended

8. and Relax

2 February 88

Summer is not going away. Today I slept in the afternoon and stayed home after not waking till three. Feeling slightly unwell, unable to put my finger on it—until I went for my second shower. Sun. Too much.

This morning I spent ten to noon in the nursery photographing the rare and elusive mauve hibiscus, and the sunshine-yellow, and huge parchment-petalled peach and ivory, the lacy white pendulous one with the blood-red centre. Waiting for the light, waiting for the breeze to fall, dizzy with the colour, dizzy from the sun, but at their peak the blossoms are compelling. Each a joy to explore, a secret moment of communion with each.

And we have to do them all. I don't know how many. Two, three hundred, and at the same time the orchids are beginning to go mad and will continue now for a long time.

But this summer business: it takes the normal passing of more than a few seasons to realize. Call some of them winter, some monsoon, but so far they have all been summer, really. And the mercury is only beginning it's upward climb. I have been here twice now through the least scorching half of the year. For a month or so I slept with a cotton cover on top of my light cotton sheet. During extreme cold I added a t-shirt, and during extreme fever, socks and a shawl.

So, new life facts: change January to August, November/December to a wet June/July, then re-invent the rest in a new spiral of heat and heavy humidity. If I survive the one you call May—the worst here—you can breathe a sign of relief and step into your own brief summer.

I will learn to wear a turban and my sisters can have my skis. Turbans are rather fetching, in any case; the slashes of colour, subtle or shocking, turn our men into tropical pirates and the women, whatever mood they feel.

The enveloping gauze fabric of the music of the santoor, woven and weighted with threads of the tabla are filling the air.

4 February 88

Welcome home. Pondy day tomorrow. A full day, with motorcycle servicing. So I will have time to look for fabric for turbans and maybe for some light dresses. It's suddenly seeming warmer somehow.

Last night, Wednesday, John dined with Barbara and joined us later for tea at Matrimandir. There. Does it feel a little different to have news now that you have a picture in your mind? We are all waiting to see if you wrote us from London. We imagined that you were well taken care of, not that anyone who has made it all the way to India and back needs taking care of at all, but company in a strange city would be nice. Our taxi trip back to Auroville was like, oh, I don't know how to say it; you were gone so FAST. But it was important that you came, for all of us. Rather a new beginning sort of feeling. I came home and sat with Desiderio for a while under his scrutiny to see if I was all right—and had you been. Then I was alone, settling in for the night, making the curd, and I caught myself wondering what to give you for lunch the next day! Funny things, aren't we.

We chose four colours of fabric for turbans, and I had lessons at breakfast in more than one variety (some only for men). I am working on perfecting the "African Knot," which even got flattering remarks from John. So I will be good and wear them.

The temperature, at 7:00 a.m. after a cold-feeling night, has been 20°C. That's apparently the coldest it's dropped here. I will check again in the day.

I think my bug (the Dengue fever) is really gone. Even my appetite is coming back, finally. And my energy level is getting more normal, but I am not pushing as hard as before. This week I will go for a bicycle ride and then take myself off the "delicate" list. The famous and amazing refrigerator will be wired for tomorrow! Eggs and heaven knows what will be added to our diet. My latest culinary triumph, requested to be repeated, daily if possible: stewed rhubarb!

I think of you happily back in your island home, trusting that you will be back here before too long. Love to everyone—did you especially thank our old neighbour for the soap?

Always, Susan

19 February 88

Then it's simple: both September and January are lovely months to begin visits. There is plenty of time between for everyone to be very ready for more company. Please just plan to come. I do miss you.

Did I tell you I bought a huge hat for picture-taking in the sun? Kidneys are holding up.

Our quiet Sunday is being interrupted by the delivery of twenty thousand unbaked bricks, which means four bullock carts, coming four or five times each, from a village nearby. They will be piled up and fired for a day and a half. Desiderio had pruned the entire compound single handed, and then four women worked all last week tying the wood into bundles, which will be used to fuel the whole process. After the bricks are cool, they will be loaded up again, and taken to two separate villages to build houses for

Radakrishna and Namudev, the gardeners, as soon as the pipes in the well are replaced (in process). It's mad, we all agree, but the cost difference is so great that it is somehow all worth it.

Still, the weather is gorgeous and I have a sewing machine for a few months, which has started me making things. I'm aiming for simple and beautiful and will test the market soon.

Details need an entire book, or to see you. All is well. With love always,

Susan

*****

This is not wanting anything or needing anything except that you know as clearly as I can tell you how I am feeling, and then just as clearly for you to say that you understand and you are happy to have me be here, or not.

I am trying to be responsible for my own well-being. Why should it feel such a risk to tell someone that you love, that you do? And that you don't want anything from them, only to have them know. And to not have it be a threat or responsibility. The way we are, which is still not always easy for me, I think is right though; it lets me feel more trust.

*****

I am whole perfect strong powerful creative loving and happy.

I am whole perfect strong powerful creative loving and happy. I am whole perfect strong powerful creative loving and happy.

*****

I struggle to translate the eyes of my friend. For me it doesn't need the fine edge of a common Mother tongue. But to pass it on, to put it outside us two, needs to go beyond the words.

*****

to know only the tone of love

to have him back in the words heard in his mother's arms.

11 February 88

Matrimandir video ideas:

The engineer walking up and through

John coming to work

Why not the emergence of several people of great variety, somehow a different image at each step?

or

Going inside—from down below

Bicycles, motorcycles arriving

Dust—heat—sun—tea—bare feet

12 February 88

Morning: Matrimandir

I pulled on shorts and t-shirt, tied my turban, and spent some hours climbing around with my camera on the first level. Mostly letting the boys get used to my being there with my camera. They did. We will all know each other better by the end of this project.

13 February 88

Saturday morning Pondy trip. We barely suppress hilarity at the deadly seriousness of the Indian merchants. Perhaps it is our combined presence. Our shopping lists land us in wildly divergent nooks and crannies of shops. But our delight is responded to, by candy pressed into our hands by the baker, handfuls of green peas and parsley thrust into our already heavy bags by the vegetable man in the bazaar. I have bought ALL his rhubarb. We will be feasting for days. Desiderio will plug in the fridge to keep the stewed treat cold. He will get used to that machine.

After the fever, a fever sort of rash, lasting longest on my legs and feet. The feet were last. Skin was tender and sensitive, and now is peeling to a fresh new foot.

Interesting, this Dengue fever. Reminds me of the dream about a layer of skin coming off, starting at my feet. Knowing I would be physically different somehow, not just smaller, afterward, and not just physically.

14/15 February

We were feeling particularly tropical at our Sunday breakfast. The weather has changed in the last few days. To wake comfortably pre-dawn, having thrown off all covers in the night, freshly blooming springtime jasmine in the air. A new orchid hung from a tree in the garden. Time for turbans and floating nothings of dresses against the mounting daytime heat. The gardener, Rangaswami, called softly at my open door to show me where he had seen our cobra. We smile at his living with us. Something sweet about their shy gentle exotic presence.

Day-long remembrances of friends and lovers.

Warm warm day. Sunday cleanup. Laundry and leisurely Sunday shower. Dinner and barefoot starlit walk. The closeness of Desiderio. Full night sky and Matrimandir from our quiet place in the amphitheatre triggered an emotional flood lasting through the night, through breakfast. He didn't laugh or make me more uneasy, but seemed to understand, relieving my distress. The feelings have persisted, but now as evening softens the day I am subdued but calm. I'm also comforted by the feeling of upheaval not seeming to be limited to me; something is in the air.

Even John, who will share my dinner, is feeling it, I think. A safe haven with his sister, he said.

Harmony: the key word. And I became afraid of the harmony I felt. Worrying for the future, "despoiling the present."

17 February

Jackals at midnight. They don't usually do that, or I don't usually hear them. Shocking, mad cacophony of overlapping crescendoing howls and then nothing—nothing—crickets again. But the echoing stays in my head. They always sound so crazed, and I've never seen them.

21 February 88

This morning I saw a vision of the Mother and Sri Aurobindo. First her eyes, which were spilling over with tears, and then the whole of Her, and Sri Aurobindo lying— his body lying—all white clothes with diamonds all around his face. She took his left hand, which was half-gloved and with diamonds, and was putting in a red rose. He was not stiff, but still life-like.

She was crying—but it was all right.

Happy Birthday.

I had earlier lit some rose incense for Her.

The climbing threatening invading white ant trails. Lightning-fast, lightning-bold evidences of their steady encroachment. The patrols for their presence grow careful, urgent. If they reach the wood...shudder. An insistent, persistent battle quietly rages.

28 February 88

Morning bonfire: birthday bonfire. Auroville's 20th. We went early, having gotten up at 4:30. This town must be reincarnated from old fishermen, no grumbling. Bed early, up and quiet tea and off in the dark. Back before breakfast to start the day again.

28 February 88

My Ashley, my sun,

Each time I see you is another lifetime. We both move and change and still always are We.

I wish we were together always, and we are.

Always,
Susan

And my father: did you know when I left that you would leave also?

To Desiderio

After this week—for both of us—with freshenings of the ache of not having those eyes the same, the same as ours to look into. To remember somehow that the love isn't lost.

I dream of holding my son, my father talks to me at night. Does he dream of holding me too?

I want to tell you now, to make sure you know, while we are here beside each other in the garden, that the light shining through you is a dear and precious gift. And if I stand beside you and not between you and IT then there can be no shadows.

You are a prince of mine from another time. You are not now a king needing a queen, but maybe you need the reassuring companionship of someone who has been quietly beside you before. I do.

Somehow this strong feeling of knowing you—much longer than this past year—helps the rest. That all is possible and nothing is lost.

Auroville's 20th birthday. Something is in the air. Maybe the immense oneness of the Universe. A divine overseeing.

Maybe we were just allowed the experience of those special children. Them needing to be received by us and held for a while in this world. Some wonderful gift of being together in that way, but not to keep. To cherish, but not to keep. Just as I would like to be cherished. It's all right. We both will understand and be all right.

I didn't mean to cry. I wanted to talk to my father and I didn't know how to find him. But I found the topaz ring he gave me, and have it on.

2 February 88

ten after two,
feeling like four,
drops of sweat on the step of the window seat bed,
where they ran off my dangling hand.

4:40 p.m.

Pruned the bohemia (the purple orchid tree), tea on the porch, in the shade for Barbara (who has a new dress), with Akash climbing trees and sweeping the leaves. I left milk for the cobra but I think the mongoose drank it.

Evening

Damp clinging silk, soothing breeze. Cooler than skin but evaporating nothing. Golden moon misted in the silvery slate night sky.

4 March 88

My nemesis has been in the garden.

The octopus cloud of her perfume in the air

stops me cold.

Wanting to see the white lotus full open in the moonlight,

I went no further.

She wasn't even there,

but had been.

5 March 88

After the full moon lull, there is a momentary suspension of tension before the new swing. Be quiet in it. Cautious inward strides.

Fill the spaces with music. I have it inside me to mix with the visions let in through my camera lens. Can I project an image of light and music playing together?

6 March 88

Dream in the night

Dressed alike from our two pairs of socks, red and yellow each, we walked into the night to bathe. When I had come back into the house after struggling along the path in the dark (stumbled, caught by branches, afraid but carried on), you were waiting for me.

Your voice was different.

You pulled me to the chair and enfolded me, kissed me. No yoga, no abstinence, giving in to male and femaleness. As you touched me I backed away, torn with not wanting us to be sorry. I loved you, I told you I was in love with you and didn't want you to go away, to stay close but wait. We went out in the night through the wet grass to the pool, long unused but somehow you had kept the water warm and clear. Plants were growing from the bottom to the surface.

You pulled me with you as you dove into the pool in an aching wanting embrace. "The next step is so close, so easy." As every cell responded to you I lost consciousness, completely.

I awakened confused, gently moving, not knowing where I was. I was outside the house, floating still. Somehow as I slept you had made a bed for me on the water and put me in. You were on the roof, watching over me, protecting me—thwarting the other man who dived in after me.

Sunday still
6 March

Learn to move through the wide-angle distortion of heat. Slowly, never mind focusing closely. Don't fall. Keep moving. It will pass.

Friday: silk sari shopping.

Saturday morning: I told him where I'd been. A smile and, "Ah, that must have been when I was considering the advantages of an Indian wife—sari shopping, for her."

For two hours I abandon myself to the yoga of laundry. Clothes off, hat on, with water poured over. Somehow it doesn't matter how long it takes. Beautiful shower place in the garden compound, follow the red brick path set into the packed red earth, winding through the swept red earth floor of the park-like setting, big neem tree, buddha belly bamboo, the jackfruit, plumerias. Pools of shade. Into the spiralled entrance to the only private outdoor place, the curved brick wall high enough that no one can see inside, trellised above, crept over with flowering vines. At last, free to disrobe, to take time for a clay mud bath, rinse off, while scrubbing the laundry with a brush, one cup of cool water to rinse the cloth, the next poured over my head, and so on.

Sunday dinner under the stars. Shining, clean, perfumed, sunburn tingle, dress for the deepening brown of skin.

Oh Sunday.

15 March 88

Quand j'ai vue Desiderio comma ça je pense que tu veux lui voir dans cette lumière. Je at 7:00 a.m. suppose que je pense de mon fils et qu'il me fait heureuse les moments de paix.

20 March 88

SPROUTS AFTER 2 DAYS = 5 INCHES WITH ROOTS.
THAT'S HOW WARM IT IS.

It seems natural that the trees here don't want to be bare for more than a day or two. This sweeping, though, is getting to be a full-time job. And the new leaves and more fabulous tree flowers come immediately. And the plumeria are reaching their peak. Now the air is even more heavy with new perfumes. Probably intensified by the intensifying heat.

No longer any reminders necessary for hat wearing; did I tell you the little white one is perfect for laundry-doing? I fill it with water first then put it on.

John, I think, is also writing today. We think it's Canada's turn but keep telling each other letters are in the mail to us! We seem to have been separately occupied lately, aside from the odd dinner together, so I went and caught him at his laundry this morning to demand a trip to the beach before dinner, when it cools down a bit (we are both fine).

Desiderio and I have thrown ourselves into studying Sanskrit. We have a teacher and actually are working like mad at it. Breakfast will never be the same. This third language between us may be the one of real communication.

Have you settled back in? Do you still feel attached to India? Let us know as soon as you think when you will be back so we can look forward to it.

We sat last night in the candlelit outdoors, ceilinged by trees, paging through picture books of British Columbia. I only got tight-throated when confronted with images of the sea, the shores where I spent so many hours, in every mood. But I managed to think how nice to have such a beautiful place be the one I came from. Desiderio touched all the pages and said he "would live there forever." Maybe someday we can come. A someday like a distant star, though, down the road a bit. I would love a picture of the plum blossoms.

28 March 88

Si tu n'a pas un autre arrangement sur ton anniversaire, puis je ferrai le cuisine tranquillement, ou, s'en irions pour le dîner si tu veux.

29 March 88

The only specific issue I want to address is the issue of Arthur's photograph.

I will not try to bother to prove to you any of my abilities. They will measure up to your criteria or they won't. I will have done my best, never having pretended to start as a professional, struggling through a difficult time when I arrived, not trying to forget it, but to find the strength to move through a series of events and failures unprecedented for me.

Now, about the photograph of Arthur. First, your derision at my saying a "bad print." Do you remember, for instance, learning to type? I personally made many errors; maybe you didn't. But the last time I was tested after a five-year absence from a machine, I managed 110 wpm.

But the thing that confused me was that when I originally showed you the shots of the little boy, you exclaimed at how lovely they were and said no, I shouldn't take the time to make a new and better copy. We must send it straight to his parents. They would appreciate it so much (also the grand-parents). I remember quite clearly writing on the back and your inserting it into an envelope for him.

Which is it? A good photo, a bad one—or something else?

I went and dug out the only copy of that print I have left. No, he isn't smiling (which is perhaps what you remember), but looking a little confused, bewildered, but a very bright, very Arthur little boy. Precisely what I saw and wanted to catch.

I understand your reserve after the last production, but even that isn't as disastrous a thing as you seem to want to cling to. A lot of those photos have been used—happily—for previously unthought-of reasons.

Reserve is one thing. And to have it voiced directly isn't comfortable, but understandable and really OK. But I found it quite inappropriate to have you say to the producer of our project—in my presence—"Oh, if only the famous French photographer were here! We all undisputedly appreciate her work."

If I had made such a statement in my gallery, said to a prospective buyer in front of a painter whose work was being considered, I would quite expect to instantly lose any rapport, respect, and paintings from that artist. I did take your statement very personally, but also couldn't help but feel a reflection on all of us as a group.

I am trying to just let it go and carry on, knowing how really concerned you are about the whole project. Do you think we are not?! And I see your enthusiasm when your eyes light up. They do. And it's lovely to see.

In the end, we need enthusiasm and creativity to continue. She will go home with the pictures and quite objectively look at each one probably a hundred times. So far she is very happy with what we've done. She feels it all will work. And so do we.

What we need now is even more a feeling of rapport and encouragement.

I would rather you had said at the beginning, "Susan, I would rather you didn't work on this."

You didn't.

Let's just get on with it.

29 March 88

Somehow here a new definition of the word "hot" is needed.

Some times I have a feeling that no other word will do. The ground is hot, too hot to walk on with bare feet. Direct sunshine magnified in the humid air is hot, motorcycle seats are hot.

But mostly what I feel is wet. Not just a little damp but dripping splashing wet. When you sleep it's not a tap dripping, it's sweat falling to the bed. The effort of writing beads the sweat on your arm and if you bend over your page it will fall off your head and smear the words.

Don't move too quickly so your senses aren't left behind in a muddled heap.

31? March 88

Marathon day: sunrise photo session with me and Matrimandir, home, shower, breakfast, Sanskrit lesson, shower, photos, home, banana dipped in gomashio, apple, tea, water, twenty minutes drenched sleep, then somehow vertical and back to work. Arrived home again and it's almost too dark to see the number lock to put cycle away. Shower, wanting sleep more than food. Artichokes just steamed encouraged a dinner built around them. Take care of me: eat, rehydrate from the day. Doze over a book. So glad it's just me to cope with.

1 April 88

Sleep is not enough. Today I will rest more, somehow. Protein.

The music I wished for was there at breakfast. A perfect enfoldment of light melodic jazz horns and plans for the day. I lingered over cool papaya. Then I touched his hand and his fingers curled round mine and their pulses somehow met—it seemed the auras merged and the pulse was one.

I have to, if I can, redefine this kind of love. I feel married, or bonded. I want to be held but not really any closer than I am. I want him to know the love I feel; maybe there will be a Sanskrit word to say the non-confusing things. That I didn't choose to fall in love. At first I thought that's all it was. It's more a recognition of someone dear—a mate to my dreams.

Why do I keep having the thought of wanting to be married? Perhaps because the husbands I had were never the companions that this one is. Because, as unattached as I am trying to be, the love is there and I want, would find it easier to relax, if there were some strong statement of recognition from him also. Not possession.

But there have been. What about this house I live in, that he gave me to live in and consider home? There has been no cause to doubt that.

Dream in the night:

Very carefully making a bed—arranging cushions, beautiful, comfortable—but not to stay there. I told the woman watching me that I had many such places, wherever I was going to be. Also an image of Desiderio's hand, clearly without the ring I had given him.

I must feel at home within myself. It is not my life to be physically grounded in one materially secure place—I am at home everywhere.

The nearness of you in the curious struggle of change and becoming is a treasured gift that I know I mustn't try to hold, but appreciate for what and how it is.

3 April

I wish I had known that the last time you and I allowed each other close enough physically to make love, that it was the last time. I think you did.

It wasn't just an episode—it isn't—but a life change that had been trying to come about, for me for a long time.

But changes that you work for (without always fully realizing why) don't announce themselves, don't ask if you are ready once they're set in motion.

Even so, I love you more than ever.

But sometimes there's a finished-with sort of feeling. I guess there's still the ego there. The part that is trying to let go of desire. After all, there is no reason; there can be no more children from me. There's been so little (from you) test of my convictions that somewhere it hurts. It should not; I should be glad that you are the same.

40
alone
celibate
Ashley is gone from me
foreign country—can't return
no money
frightened

*****

nearly 40: the best is coming
free
harassment is over

4 April 88

In this climate, the wine we had at dinner last night turned into a heavy depressant. Dredged up every doubt and misgiving.

For me, now, half a bottle of wine is not interesting.
I am
whole perfect strong powerful creative
Loving and

Happy

I release this situation

And

Everything connected

With this

Situation

and

I ask for

GUIDANCE

7 April 88

Deep sadness—tears never far from the surface—sometimes leaking out. Why?

Is it this project-finishing and feeling rootless? And the roots I do have are meeting rocky hard ground?

It's an alone feeling, trying to feel comfortable in this supposed Oneness where all the bits like molecules are banging into each other, angry, scared. Toughen, strengthen.

Wandered Pondy alone at the height of heat. Most of the shops I wanted were closed.

8 April 88

Quick letter being mailed in America:

Desiderio asks that I send you a kiss.

We have finished shooting for the video. This is going with the woman who is putting it all together. She was here with us for three weeks from Colorado, and we have been working incessantly. Now I will take a few days and rest.

Your picture of the tour guide in London practicing crowd control was wonderful, I thought. Worthy of a blow-up and framing. Amused me to no end.

The taxi is about to come for our filmmaker. We are all madly addressing envelopes to go.

The birds under the banyan are deafening.

Much love and a proper letter soon,

Susan

10 April 88

New curd, milk from beautiful new cow. Smooth, firm, incredible texture of crème caramel. A Swiss starter, we think. The oddest things smuggled from Europe.

Now all we need is caviar for Desiderio. I was trying to get it in time for his birthday, but the manifesting of the new beginning of milk delivery was a joy.

14 April 88

Today I started working IN Matrimandir.

Aside from the fact that we are working near the ceiling in the Chamber, getting the bolts ready for the marble to go on the walls, it's a grounding time.

I've thought it over—briefly.

It is an alone feeling. Why am I not strong enough not to occasionally want some special person to come and say, "I'm glad you're home, can I come and sit with you awhile? I only just felt like being close to you."

Does it ever cross your mind to do that, and are there reasons you don't, or don't you think of it? I think you don't.

Why does this feeling of loneliness keep sweeping over me? It comes and goes.

You do share with me already a lot, and the best time of the day. The beginning and the end on Sundays, which are dear to me. But I feel time-slotted, allotted, permitted at those times, and then—and then what? I feel like the other half of someone else; that that's how you see me. I am not the other half of anyone. Not her, not you, not my brother even.

I am a whole part of this one thing.

I just must trust that this is my rightful place in the Universe and if it needed someone else to be in this spot, someone else would have been put here. I never wanted to just glide along and be content with an easy but wrong path, and now I am in tears because I am a little tired, warm, away from familiar things and feeling lonely. Everyone here in Auroville is in the same boat. I was pulled here because it needs me too. To help, not to be snowed under and give up. Not to be sad or frightened. To be the bright, creative, enthusiastic person that I am. Susan.

Sunday

I never dreamed that when I entered this stage of my life, the alone part, that there would be someone so sometimes-close that my heart would want to break from memories of long-ago sweetness.

How can you tell someone who is trying to be a hermit that you are plagued with periodic bouts of being lonely? How can you tell them that without jeopardizing their friendship or threatening their right to aloneness (which you yourself value)?

I can't very well come to you on days when I feel that way in case you may think I feel it all the time. And it's not just any company.

If I could have come days ago and said, oh give me a hug and a cup of tea. But don't you see, it feels like an intrusion.

And of course I should tell you because you aren't insensitive and there's nothing you can do except know. I feel like I'm here to conquer all my emotions and they are strong. The loving ones aren't a problem. It's the lonely one I don't understand.

19 April 88

What I need to experience I am experiencing.

20 April 88

Final consonants are not pronounced except:

C R F L (Careful)

Est-ce que je donne?

Est-ce que je no donne pas?

Donnes-tu?

Est-ce que tu donnes?

Est-ce que tu ne donnes pas?

Pouvez-vous me dire ou se trouve la poste? Là-bas

Par ou est-ce?

Par ici

Par la

Par la-bas

C'est par ici.

C'est par la-bas.

Je ne veux pas y aller.

Oui, je le suis.

This way

That way

Over that way it's this way

It's over that way

Non, je ne le suis pas.

21 April 88

Week one: working on Matrimandir. Our women's team is still gung ho. We are now getting the cement mixer cleaned for painting. Not all one colour. It's going to look like a giant ice cream machine by the time we're finished!

Nursery: plumeria catalogue photoing. While focussing on a group of red rubia, light reflected down from the silvery branches and white blossoms above and behind, swimming the whole background into an underwater mirage.

A step into Atlantis. That's all it takes, a glance at the right moment.

1 May 88

The truth may be always fine, but if, in hearing it, someone backs away, the results of the expression may be temporarily a blow. But having taken the risk exposes their truth.

Just another life change.

1 May 88

Last night after dinner I finally just told Desiderio all the things of loving and of my feeling that he was more of a mate or even husband than anyone had ever been.

And then today, Sunday, when we normally have dinner, there was no invitation. I thought he was very gently backing away. I coped with it.

Then he came. Where was I? '"You didn't invite me."

"I didn't see you all day; dinner is nearly ready."

No false pique, no drama. It would have been a game, which we don't play. Except the ones for fun.

He had spent the afternoon reworking the necklace for his symbol to include the amber bead I had given him yesterday.

He has not rejected me. Or my truth.

3 May 88

My heart is pounding with the thunder. This storm-building excitement is in every atom.

After the—for once—charmless madness of Pondy this morning, to be insulated in a candlelit haven, unseasonal rain washing away all outside sounds, cool breeze swaying my crystals in the open windows, catching diamonds from the small dancing flames that I've been reading by.

In the energetic flurry after actually finishing my Sanskrit homework, as the storm built, I wrote a dinner invitation to Desiderio. In Sanskrit. But as it got darker and wetter and wilder outside, I became more concerned with his homecoming being made easier. Some worry that he would be caught in a flood. He was.

He was too wet, cold, tired, and as the rain turned me inside myself I became happier and happier to be alone.

At 8:15 I am luxuriously in bed with chai, book, all my candles around, cool enough to really want to be in my bed. It seems so long since I've wanted to be covered.

6–7 May 88

The night dream

Full of pain consciously inflicted, and endured, and stopped. Scars will be there. Injustices of crimes, resigned to with no seeming resentment. Unequal treatment of prisoners—but still captive.

Sunday

Even though my door is always open to you I am not waiting for you to walk through it.

11 May 88

Tuesday, Pondy late afternoon trip to the ashram. Samadhi. As we walked in and left our shoes, put down our bags, I clearly and immediately heard a voice saying, "Let go of all the pain, of everything that is hurting you. There is no need."

I cried softly standing at the rail.

12 May 88

Am I adding to your coolness when I come for some brief reason in the evening by expecting it and taking care not to come too near you, or say too much, and thinking in advance that you don't want to be disturbed or approached for anything because you have had enough in the day?

I remember you saying once last year that it wasn't very often that you wanted to see someone.

Is it part of my *sadhana* to always try to be understanding of the needs of people and acquiesce to their wishes, and to not have needs or wishes of my own?

What about me? What do I need?

13 May (a.m.)

Wait a minute. It is a cycle—my biological cycle that triggers these feelings.

Before getting supramentalized I give myself permission to clear up one vital thing: my nemesis.

Either speak to me or don't. But be consistent, because soon I won't trust at all the beautiful sweetness that you show sometimes. I'm not sure if you show it when you're able, or at your convenience.

21 May 88

At dinner, for a moment, I saw nothing but loving in your eyes, open and undisguised. We turned back to our homework.

He had made ice cream to surprise me.

25 May

Tonight when we came home I had been fighting and trying not to fight, just let go, of wanting to sleep beside you, have you near. I tried to think of other things. And then you pulled nostalgia from me and now I am left suspended between two things I cannot have and feel I must not want.

I don't know if you feel those things. I don't know if it's only me struggling alone with it.

The last time I came to you in the night was only because there was physical pain I couldn't manage. Emotional needs are somehow to be conquered.

26 June 88

A call—a pull—to be inside your aura. To feel the universe from the circle of your arms. With the blending of our colours, your blood flows in my veins and your tears fall from my eyes. Our breathing slows and rhymes.

You pulled me to you so I could know the tears.

27 June 88

Thank you. How sweet and unexpected. My money does seem to be holding out much better than even hoped for. But cushions are always so comforting.

Large writing because it's hot and we're all tired after surviving last week, which built up to and culminated with a nineteen-hour concreting from 3:00 p.m. John was heroic and is OK. Yesterday he skipped an afternoon meeting to take me to the beach. Knock-you-down-and-bowl-you-over kind of waves, and strong current. Perfect.

One of the men has been "out-of-station" for about a month, and says we've all lost weight. I guess we have, but are taking extra care to eat well, making everything count. So I think we are all healthy, just melting away in puddles.

A Pondy evening, again. The weeks roll by so quickly. We will only cope with necessary things and dinner (with a COLD beer) and get the heck out of there.

I am getting John trained to come for dinner not just when I think to ask him, but whenever he feels like it—nice and relaxed. Got to shower and go.

with my love always, Susan (and from Desiderio, who asks after you often)

1 July 88

The dog is dead. Chien. He was nobody's dog, but in the end he was ours.

This morning, walking across to breakfast, I thought, when the dog goes, please don't let me be the one to find him. I won't know what to do. And then, as we sat, the screaming horn of the lorry hurting my ears, hurting Chien. We didn't know. Poor old thing, skinnier and uglier every day—but sweet and loving somehow.

What a relief for him at last to be able to lie down with no pain.

5 July 88

Day after the fourth of July. American Aurovilians did not go to the embassy in Madras as they normally would for the holiday celebration.

Yesterday the Americans blew up an Iranian airplane: three hundred passengers, seventy-five of them children.

Today my cold and fever hang on. In the morning I asked Desiderio to take me to the beach, for medicinal purposes. By afternoon I had a strong feeling that we or he should go to the village instead and check on our gardener friend. I felt trouble. I thought about how you can't always help someone else's life—you can't.

DDT

*****

Pulse of a scene,
seen through a screen.
Trees move with my heartbeat,
the wind blows my mind.
Segmented fragmented, so clearly connected.

9 July

I want to be held like you're going to hold that child. And so do you. There's a heart-ripping scream of abandonment inside.

Watch it, hear it; you are not that.

Ashley c/o Mom

I'm hoping you're there. Hoping you're coming. I haven't heard—not a word.

9 July 88 (aerogramme)

I'm hoping Ashley's there with you, or hoping he's coming. There's nothing I can do from here but trust that you two will have some contact. Take pictures of each other, write a letter, send a tape, talk to each other.

Two frogs are sitting on the desk watching me write this. The other day one jumped off the bookcase and landed on my face! They are small and sweet and funny, and I saw him coming and I still jumped. Soft and cool.

The kids here are just going back to school. Summer holidays are earlier because of the HEAT.

We have all managed to catch summer colds and fevers. Not life-threatening or worth a trip to the nursing home, but they have slowed us right down for a few weeks. At least no trouble "sweating it out." We are OK now!

My table and bench outside are underway. The bench under the tree close to the house has had its edges rounded by the stonemason (twenty-five rupees) and the bench will be an oval three quarters around, with a curved and sloping back. It will be built with bricks (I am helping). Then tiles will go on after. Another week or so and I can eat and study outside. The workers are teaching me to count in Tamil, and a friend is here from France just now so my French is improving a little. We have tea with the dictionary between us.

Still waiting for the rain,

Susan

10 July 88

Ah, good morning. Sweet Sunday again in the City of Dawn. We've all made it through the night again.

Somewhere in the night, speaking to my father, someone had died. The third time in dreams this week.

I didn't want him to do anything for me, just to know I was struggling harder for a little while.

*****

a wave of dawns

a continuous crescendoing

    dawning

spiralling time

Cities of dawn.

11 July

I wish once more in this lifetime, just once even, to spend a whole night in your arms. And not when someone is not feeling well, or is sad, or frightened, but just for the love of it. For the love of you—and knowing there will never be another man.

Would there be? The question.

17 July 88

last night—after Madras trip—dream

The ocean coming together while I was standing out there. The huge wave. My dinner floating just under the surface—got it. The old man stage director said he had seen it done before and

wondered how. But it was at the end of an act—an illusion—and we were doing it in the middle.

The mail arrived: great pile of envelopes and small parcels, cheques, letters from friends. The means and openings for me in hand, to do whatever I wished. I was going somewhere—or wanting to go.

22 July 88

Last midnight walking home after the rain, silent strobe flashes of lighting. This morning, a suffused glow of a cloud covered the dawn. The air is cool enough to add a strong swelling music to the domestic chore time before work. Bodies relishing the breezes, an illusion of temperature freshness.

The other morning when I was happily getting ready for work, with no thought of leaving here in my head, I realized I can't. That there is somehow an unspoken commitment to be here with John, for the duration. Oh, not that I can't, but the consideration would be huge. And it's all OK.

I thank you every day for the peppermint foot crème, still, for my hands. I've been working with concrete. My beautiful table outside and the bench around it is nearly done.

Please give my love to everyone I miss. It's a big list, play it by ear.

22 August 88

On days when your days are too much I only want to be a quiet place for you. Even if that means staying away, or not telling you the feelings that I want to.

28 August 88

Dear Mom,

Whatever did happen to long lazy summers? I guess it's been long and lazy alright but only on the outside. Inside it's been full-speed.

Are you surviving your month with the grandchildren? I imagine those two are fairly independent by now and likely self-occupying. I hope you know how relieved and happy I am that Ashley could come to you. Without that tie I find it hard. But knowing you can see him, and tell me that he's alright, lets me breathe more easily. I know there's probably a lot he doesn't say about things being tough. But I think, not just because he's mine, that he will somehow be more than OK.

My bench is finished today. We used red terra-cotta tiles with natural-coloured cement and smooth little pebbles in the gaps. The whole thing is a phenomenon that kept changing a little as it grew and grew. It is extremely hand-made (but well), with input from me, Desiderio, Namudev, and Radakrishna. Makes you smile.

Now Colette comes from Paris, and will sit at it in the shade with tea and a book, or a friend,

as though it's always been there.

I have moved into Desiderio's house for the duration of her stay. We've had a week to cope with the change before her arrival. WE are fine with it (after I got over a nervous rash starting a few days before the changeover). I will report at the end of the month or in five or six weeks!

My income tax return arrived. $393. Nice of them.

All this company and moving are conspiring to shoot our study time all to pieces. But our teacher says that taking care of visitors in the Indian culture is very important work. She taught us the Sanskrit word for it, and understood. I think partly she just enjoys our "class" of two.

> To be continued...with my love, Susan

28 August 88

You are on your way back to the airport after an intense sister visit. For a month, we've been seen as triplets, a step up from the twin-ness of John and I. Too much talk to do any writing at all.

Funny, that feeling when I held you that last moment—instant and total consumption with not wanting to let you go—a swift pain of blood pulling from me. And then to release you into a swirling universe—gone—like an orbiting star that won't stop shining out of view.

I will feel the tremble of our paths crossing and recognize the sisterhood of it, if it takes a year or ten or a thousand.

Day after

Labour Day

Your footsteps

my Heartbeat.

7 September 88

Ramu, Ina, Ingeborg

White-blond West German hair soft against her pale yellow skin and eyes. Resting trustingly on my lap, her frail pale yellow body stretched limply in the back seat of the taxi to Pondy.

I put my friend in the nursing home by the sea. Hepatitis has struck another one of us down. In the white, bright room her jaundiced look intensifies. The doctor has said she is very sick.

9 September 88

last night, the dream

In the evening, walking down the street with the man. My man.

We were to be alone for several days for the first time. His wife and children were away. As we reached a big old house, with steep stairs, he picked me up in his arms and carried me up.

His friend said, "That's a first." The man said, "Yes, it's the first time I could. I show her what expression of love I am able to each time. She is mine." Inside my head, close to his ear, I said "Then make love to me."

13 September 88

Thursday

Entry group, Ganesh puja

Friday

Colette, for you I wish I could speak to you more and for me that I could understand each word you say. To even be able to say why I went to business college instead of university. Or not simply, no, I don't play any music nor paint, but maybe what I do feel strongly about.

*****

We admire the determination of little creatures. The determination of plants to bloom and bear fruit. Their delirious spurts of growth after a tropical storm.

This morning in the garden, on a blade of grass, I found (because I was looking for a four-leaf clover) a strikingly beautiful black and white cocoon. Looking as closely as I could, I wasn't sure if it was a caterpillar waiting to make its cocoon or the butterfly waiting for the strength to unfold itself.

*****

Shadowy eucalyptus under a bleak grey sky. Cathedral quiet of the ancient mango grove. Stained glass mottles to move through and lean against, and talk quietly or not at all. The strong old trunks.

And the banyan forest creeping to surround the Shiva temple. One tree, the original trunk long ago lost.

19/20

night dream

You were lying an arm's length away from me and took my hand and pulled me to you, saying, "Come here, I want you close to me." I felt my heart constrict and tears come as I told you you'd never said that before.

25 September 88

There's no photo of me but somehow I will try to make one of me or someone. It means going into the shower at about five o'clock; the sun shines in that particular angle through the trellis overhead. You look in the mirror while washing your hair and find that water droplets have clung to your eyelashes, turning the pupils of your eye to crystal.

Saturday

My heart is spinning slowly—thickly—banging on my skin from the inside, aching in my chest and pushing tears out my eyes.

Humid dappled sunshine and birdsongs are pressing from the outside.

9 October 88

Listen: I will tell you—because I think you want to hear— if saying no, no to old lovers who still wanted me with them, if saying to friends who wanted more than I could give, if you care for me enough to stay and be my friend—only that—then stay because I value your friendship, but otherwise, go from me.

My life has changed, just further down the road it had been going.

And to my mother I explained, in a half-year of explaining many things, that you somehow just fitted with me. Above caring if we ever were lovers again, even though you were the sweetest man ever I had felt the nearness of. That you made me cry with the homecoming of a thousand years, lying in your arms.

If you find no joy in relationships—what then? What then, because I needed a home? Because there is a companionship that doesn't pressure you too much? I don't believe there is no love from you, come to think of it. I also don't believe you find no joy—maybe barely, maybe quietly, but I have seen it, again and again.

20 October 88

Can you imagine this garden? Each day I am struck by some new thing. A few days ago the philodendron creeping down from the jackfruit tree was swinging just above my head and then would brush my neck as I walked by. And now it is down past my shoulders. The bougainvillaea that partly trellises the shower is sending yards-long shoots straight into the sky.

Colette et René

Déjà je regard en avant a la prochaine fois que vous serez ici, il était un peu solitaire quand vous nous laisse.

Mais plus d'une fois j'ai vu et parler avec vous dans la nuit, le langage n'a semple pas un problème.

Quand je porte les améthystes, je sera conscient de leur protection et la chaleur de ton embrassement.

*****

Isn't it the inconvenient nature of emotions that they usually are held or flow in an emotional way? When I got home the truth of what I had said to you through tears was still there. But the tears of it, the ache of it, just let go.

You laughed at me at the right time and held me at the right time in the right way.

I am not sad. I just had let pile up too many small circumstances, forgetting for a moment all the warm and lovely moments of my day.

30 October 88

Your birthday card, note, and most welcome photos arrived in thirteen days flat—well, not flat exactly, open on three sides, a bit bent, with a big rubber band around it. Do you have a copy of the picture of Ashley from four years ago of him standing in the carport looking at a ball in the air just above his hand? (He looks like a Norman Rockwell model to me.) It is an amazing thing to look at it beside the one you just sent of him juggling. I will frame them together.

Did John (or I) say that John says it feels like looking at his own face?

Where are you going to that you are taking a note-taking seminar?! A big trip? Where, where, where? Feels like it must be going to be an adventure. I am so glad for you. But when, where, and how long?

Yesterday I couldn't write because I had a prisoner. The gardener caught a young boy cutting bougainvillea in the driveway; he also had his cows with him. I was home. Desiderio wasn't. So I had to keep him till the man of the house came home. Oh, his father came also; we stood between to avert a beating on the spot and made him stay for the day and work in the garden and made his father, who had said, "Yes, he's a bad boy, I don't want him, take him to the police," agree not to beat him after and go find the cows himself (by this time gone for two hours). I was trying to be serious, overcome with the absurdity that in a country of eight hundred million, the six hundred of us have the audacity to take prisoners.

All the while, three carpenters finishing the window screens in my house.

I will tell you about the lightning hitting and completely killing the tree ten feet from my house—with me standing there—another time.

love always, Susan

3 November 88

I just stopped and ate a huge bowl of soup. I was freezing cold, with a slight sore throat; I came home with a chill at noon. The temperature has suddenly dropped to 27°C. I guess when your body gets used to the world feeling the same inside and outside, any drop at all is a rude shock.

My dear friend Marlenka has a banyan tree that started as a bonsai in a pot. She wants to liberate it. Desiderio says OK—we can have it. What joy! Imagine having two of those in the garden. We'll be taken over. Great!

13 November 88

I think the only thing to call this is an approach-to-a-fortieth-birthday crisis.

Wednesday
16 November 88

40th birthday

When you gave me the ring in my dream, you said that I could wear it on my left hand, knowing the bonding of it. I almost asked if you realized that you had married me in the night.

The Tibetan turquoise is warm against my skin and I can feel you in it.

25 November 88

I went through a half-day (only) of (serious) fortieth birthday trauma the Sunday before and now feel the happiness, strength, and freedom in that milestone. I thought very much of you during the day. The birth of your first child and the following sequences of events for both of us.

I seem to have become attached as photographer to Auroville's new newspaper. I like the people and the way they work together. A group managing any sort of creative process is a near-miraculous thing. I will slip you onto the mailing list.

Have you gone away?

Next time you come we must have a "Plan B" and even "C" in case of late planes and missed connections. We always hope for things to go as smoothly as your visit, but sometimes we just get reminded more strongly that this is India.

With love, always, Susan

12 December

Feeling like leaving. Nowhere to go.

14 December

I suppose the rhythm of things, of the natural cycle of things in women, most obviously in me, isn't something that can be controlled, more just to be aware of.

Even though there are these few rougher days that seem to require a little more understanding and patience or maybe one more hug, the days of balance on the other side more than compensate. Not needing, not wanting anything, but a wide-open nurturing love just passes through and cannot be diminished; it only grows more and more the more it lands on.

That is always there, and I am so glad when you laugh at me so sweetly.

25 December 88

Here I sit contentedly ground to a halt. Smack in the middle of my housework. Feet up with tea and a book—door and windows all are open with a springy breezy breeze blowing around cooling my skin. And even the book eased out of being read as the afternoon slant of sun caught the lazily turning crystal hanging in the window.

Each late afternoon the sun rays find their way through the dappled green of trees behind, shooting starfire from the bevelled teardrop.

29 December 88

An intrusion!

I cannot imagine a time when I would feel it an intrusion if you came to see me.

I liked it when you would come sometimes and sit with me, or when you came with chocolate for us.

But now I realize that either it just doesn't occur to you anymore, or it does and you choose not to.

1 January 89

This year I will find the way of loving you freely that does not want anything. Not support or companionship that isn't absolutely voluntarily given, and to accept that your support may not come in the way that I think I want it.

And to let it happen without becoming cold or cynical.

14 January 89

Why is it that the last lover I had—or had me—I dreamed in the night (as he held me) that he died, peacefully. And I knew it was all right; it had been saying goodbye.

*****

Sometimes, like this morning when I ask you too many questions that you can't or won't answer, you look so hurt, so lost, that I wish I could take them back and simply be there quietly beside you, asking nothing from you and letting you be...and never ever hurting you and just being someone you can trust for a lifetime.

I'm sorry if I push you sometimes, but you did ask for me to be here, so you must have known somewhere I would do that.

20 March 89

if you can only
  come to me
dans la nuit
when part of me
  is sleeping
  then we do it that way.
Not two lives
  One full one.

21 March 89

Butterfly flutter of bamboo as the rising sun shifts the morning breeze. Surreal startle of the desert rose insists a fourth dimension to the silver grey-green spires and spokes of my cactus garden. The lifting mists, the visibly raining dew of our cool days—gone. Now only a vague haze burned even by the first piercing rays of dawn.

Circles of weeks—an imperceptible spiral

Ascending—widening

Till the boundaries of self dissolve through stars

25 May 89

Yesterday (24 May 1983) was the sixth anniversary of the bus crash that sent me off on a new path. My choice to live—fully.

This morning I woke with a lovely sense of well-being.

27 May 89

I am sending you my address so that for sure you know where I am.

This is not to disrupt your life, your family days, not to shake you. I am grateful that your new wife is there with you and always have been.

I am putting your name and Ashley's on the subscription list of our small newspaper; over the months it will perhaps give you all some idea of life here. I race around on my cycle and do most of the photos.

I never wished to be separated from our son and don't feel that I am. But geographically, it's been a problem from the first. When I know that he is all right, I am all right.

I am grateful for your steady companionship of him. I always saw that you adored him, and needed him actually with you. I can't tell you how many times I ached to "grab him and run" or tried to figure how we would together make it work, but I knew that if I took him—if I just one day kept him—he would be glad to be with me but would worry to death about you. And that you would be frantic. It is not something I am trying to hold, or take; he is every day my son. Yes, of course, and yours, and even his new mother's too.

I have had to trust all along that the bond of birth and the first precious years when he and I were so together was something that would not break.

I believe that Ashley came to you and I for a reason, as divergent as our lives have turned out to be. Perhaps because of that, perhaps it widens his scope. He can dream anything from one end of the world to the other, because of us. He will not be limited.

I think it is important for you and me to cooperate and retain or regain some contact to encourage him in everything and anything he may wish for.

I don't want him to be afraid of loving, for instance, because it can cause pain and walls. It need not.

Please, please don't let the contact with my mother lapse, even if it means phoning her collect or asking her to pay to have him come and visit. She will do that.

30 May 89

I don't know if I'm big enough yet to not care if there is some one person close by who is not beyond telling me occasionally that he cares that I am there.

I keep trying to be.

Should I?

There must be a solution to this. What can I do with this feeling, this ache of tears? I wanted to work until I just fell asleep, but there's not enough light. I can't.

Ride this one out and hope it's the moon...

the moon is true

but it's blue

just read your book

and back to work in the morning.

22 June 89

Survived the summer solstice—but did we all?

25 June 89

Last night I said to Desiderio, as we sat in the spaceship table under the wind-whirled tree canopy, a candlelit envelope in the warm night (we were Sunday-night clean, and fed and leaning easily on each other), "It feels like you are becoming, or I am realizing that you are, a true companion to me—as though, imagine: not a fairy tale, but in that time, that sometimes you had to go off and fight a dragon, or I did, or maybe both of us, and then once in a while, we would both come home to the castle, to rest in a safe place, in front of the fire, and it's a quiet place. Sometimes even one of us is wounded and the other takes care." He smiled in the dark and pulled me companionably closer.

6 July 89

Start working in the office, Matrimandir.

17 August 89

Finish. Agree to go one time/week.

22 August 89

Last time.

10 September 89

red coral: stimulates the energetic pursuit of pre-determined goals – protects from depression and despondency.

21 September 89

This is a new day. I don't know how strong I am, or how alone I am.

Last night I dreamed of not being able to see or walk or speak and then I fell to the ground and finally was only able to call once for help.

22 September 89

Why am I here? A day like this seems a good day to ask.

When it's still too hot, when a close friend of years has come and gone again (perhaps for years and years), back to the other side of the world that I felt compelled to launch myself from.

From one of the most lovely natural areas of this world. So it was a pull, the idealism of dreams and a sprouting hope for something I knew could not be foreseen.

I don't remember actually ever actively making a decision to come here, and most certainly not to stay. Suddenly it just WAS the only important thing in my life to come, and obstacles fell out of the way. And then arriving—I was home. As simply as that.

But more than being home, a mysteriously strong feeling of responsibility to be part of this experiment. Knowing I am small and not so strong.

Friday
29 September 89

Since yesterday, Desiderio is down. Flat. Tonight I am so grateful to be able to say to him, "Be careful, I see a smile cracking through." Grey still sky. Fighting fevers. Everyone.

30 September 89

Woke last night from just falling asleep unable to remember how to spell my name. Clearly, my father's voice saying, "Susan, Susan." Thanks.

Work out in the morning. Attentiveness to the physical rhythms is grounding—or is it grounding, exactly?

We came for some of the myriad human reasons that people emigrated always. But not better material living conditions, certainly not a more gentle climate than that of our births.

Sometimes, some days, it's been too hot for too long, drought is beyond a threat, the details of our days become a tedious struggle.

6 October 89

I am strong, and not alone.

Sunday
9 October 89

Small crisis after good strong calm morning, mid-afternoon through dinner, about being taken for granted.

Friday
20 October 89

Acupuncture

Haircut by Desiderio

28 October 89

Water falling through blossom-scented air.

Darker and greener and glistening. Now candle time and a shawl and curl on my bed with a book and tea. I want to sleep in this waterfall murmur, but I want to watch it fall; it hasn't rained for so long.

It feels cosy and private; no one moves in this much.

Sunday
Mid-January 1990

Time for me to hold the fort. It's my turn for however long it takes.

Last night, the dream: swimming, learning to swim out past the incoming waves, not to be crashed, just ride through them.

6 February 90

Lost, the last four days. Trying to manage. Lonely but feel like hiding, sad, feel like crying.

Maybe just take a good nap.

6th night

The dream: very pregnant, past due, bleeding a bit. It stopped. Someone said to me, "Could have had it on my birthday." Waiting. Knew I would be alone. A little afraid but knew it was all right, I had done it before.

7th morning

Stormy in the air. Wind, few rain drops. Next time depression hits check the barometer. Lifted suddenly.

I will stop the newspaper work. I spoke with a cohort; she concurs. Leave like a princess.

8 February 90

Breakfast announcement: in all conscience, whether or not I have some other secure thing to do, I must leave the newspaper work. Circumstances have changed, me too.

It will be all right, time to trust that.

Later this same morning, while delivering Janet's second window hanging, she asked me to come work with her.

Afternoon 5ish

I tell her yes, but let's start gently. We will talk next week.

Friday/Saturday

Full moon—eclipse

Sunday
February 11ish

Last night dream: John had carved a totem for me. At the bottom, himself as a small boy smiling hugely, arms above his head holding a giant fish. He cemented it into the ground in front of my house as we were getting ready to go to the beach.

I was carrying him, the small boy. Someone asked if he was heavy. I said to them, "He's not heavy, he's my brother."

Laughing at that when I wake.

26/27 (night)

Dream of whales playing in the waves at the beach. I met a woman from Orcas island, and for the first time realized the name is of those whales. One got caught in a breaker; unable to escape, it was flipped onto the beach. Huge black tail crashing down. I couldn't move. "I may be killed," but I sat still, and it missed my outstretched feet by inches or so.

27 February 90

Cycled to the beach.

28 February 90

Auroville's 28th birthday

Working on my own now, gently.

Desiderio down since two days ago. On the night before he fell into this blue funk, I had a dream fragment in which, somehow, someone had slipped a BAD THOUGHT into the neighbourhood. Do you realize what that means? That someone can possibly hurt us that way—like a disease? Is Desiderio under attack?

1–2 March

As Desiderio climbs from his depression (a little), I fall in (a lot). Keep track.

I also forget this menopause business. Better check.

19 March 90

Suddenly it's all worth it again.

20 March 90

I am feeling quietly strong and happy, and ready again to dive into my life; when I dream, I dream of diving into the ocean.

Si tu m'avais demander encore une fois si je suis heureuse, il faut que je dit—oui.

La crise des semaines et des mois passé sont casser. J'ai essaye a rester calme et laisse passer toutes les vagues, all the crashes autour de moi.

Il faut que j'apprendre la différence des sentiments que viennent. There is the salt sweet gift of friendship, of caring, that never can be experienced without distance in physical time and space. It is to know that it doesn't matter—there is really no such thing as any kind of separation—I feel joyful and strong.

21 March 90

The immediate intimacy of feelings are not a desire for attachment, but something to be explored and treasured as a gift. This is a wonderful mystery to me.

later

I have written to you both more than once and destroyed the letters, because I didn't want to bring anything difficult for you.

This is about "the money." Please, I know it isn't your problem or responsibility, or part of our friendship. It's just that so often when I could really use it—when I think of being able to come home for a visit, or to make it more easy here, I remember that debt.

Mostly, I have let go any hope of recovering it.

If I wanted to come back and stay there, my mother would manage it, I'm sure. But a visit is a different thing; that, I don't feel free to ask for.

I don't know where your daughter is or her situation now, but she had been so adamant that the money would be in my hands when I left that I believed her. Three thousand dollars for me, here, would go a VERY long way.

If you have any contact with her and can bring it up without a torment to yourselves I would be grateful.

I will say nothing to my mother of this so there won't be any uneasiness.

I think of you all so often. Mom is always sending "Hellos" from people she bumps into. Our days in the restaurant kitchen were such good preparation for here for me: the heat, no water, no electricity or supplies. It's a fond memory somehow, still. I love you all.

PS: If you manage to wrench it out of her, a bank draft should be sent in US funds. Our bank here is most reluctant to handle Canadian dollars.

My fingers are crossed—please drop me a note in any case.

love still,

Susan

22 March 90

I will save all the thoughts running through me today and let them settle.

Rose shadows
Pale blue hint of a bloom.

later

Dear Mom,

I will go to Singapore to meet Ashley! Oh, thank you for including that one line tacked onto the end of your last letter. Imagine, our boy, winning an essay contest with a prize to Singapore and Thailand! That's going to be some journey, with one student from each of the school districts in British Columbia being chosen. What on earth could he have written about?

There are several ways I can fit into that wonderful plot.

a. Get all the information. Reach the organizers (school?) and lump in with the chaperones, getting to and from Singapore on my own. That should help my case for joining them, I hope.

b. Get the information and simply meet their flight. There are many people here with friends in Singapore.

I showed your letter to Desiderio, with heart pounding. He said "PACK NOW!" "There's time to figure it all out; we have three months!" Neighbours had the same response. When, to John at dinner, I expressed doubts of barging in, he said "Nonsense. They will be having so much fun that you will be just one more element of fun."

I want to read his essay. I will write to him in a day or two. Gently, not to spook anyone. If you can dig up details for me, I would be eternally grateful. What a lucky break that you had a letter returned and happened to catch him on the phone.

I will try to sleep, and write again in a day or so.

I think your plans for renovating your house to have a painting studio and guest room are terrific! Room for a visit from John in '91?

Thanks, Mom, of course you should have spilled the beans. That's your grandson to be proud of—and my baby!

Always love, Susan

12 April 90

Under the filtered shadow of these amoebas swimming around, nothing hurts, the music of life still goes on—but in a sultry lower octave and more often the blues. Not sweet blues, blue ones. It makes me want to go home. I don't feel like fighting it anymore. The struggle of my day is to keep from crying.

26 April 90

Dear Mom,

I am busy working, surviving the heat wave, and waiting for news from that end. I checked my journal just now and realize that it is hardly physically possible to have had a letter back, but then, did my letters get there? I have written to Ashley—with the correct postal code finally—mostly just congratulations, not to panic anyone with the thought that I intend to see him. Oh, why should that panic anybody?

I am trying to take for granted that he will just be as happy to see me as I will be to see him, because I know it's really true, and not worry about the rest of it.

The thermometer in the day, in the shade, now reads about 39°C. Friends at the Guest House tried to find out about the sunshine temperature, but the thermometer only went to fifty. When it got to forty-eight and was still wanting to rise rapidly, they grabbed it in. Barbara figured it was about seventy-five. That's 167°F. We think she was right. Yes, wear a hat. But we are all still vertical, except during rest time in the afternoon (when we are all horizontal). Me, in my hammock under the trees with the little breeze.

Two proven cures for sunstroke, which would be good to remember even there, are aspirin and gin. That's what all those Englishmen were drinking it for. That and it's also good against amoebas, apparently (as is any alcohol). For the sunstroke, one gin or one aspirin will do.

Is your house all finished? I think it must be very nice. I tried to explain your diagram to John. I dream of the beach sometimes.

It gets increasingly difficult in this long summertime to do any creative sewing—or anything. Desiderio thinks we get points for just making it through the days. So my "office time" during the week does sort of balance it, even if while we are there the current can be off five times in the morning, or something goes wrong with the computer while the power IS on. Seems to be part of my work to keep them calm.

Meanwhile, we are having a wonderful time in the garden. Veeramangai, who has worked in the garden here for maybe eight years, has again, at last (and forever this time) been fired. She was like facing the Wicked Witch of the West every day; no racism about it, it was her personality. Now everyone is so happy and it doesn't seem she will be replaced. She didn't do much anyway. It had gotten so traumatic that Desiderio was paying her for a full day on the condition that she GO AWAY at one o'clock. Can't help but laugh; she was winning. So now the garden is more cared for than ever. She wasn't the gardener. Radakrishna, Rangaswami, and Namudev do that; all the bunding and big watering and heaven knows what else, but they practically live here. SO, each day now at the end of the afternoon, you can find one or up to four of us at a time joyfully sweeping. That means with those short bundle-of-straw brooms, and do you remember HOW BIG our garden is? That includes sweeping the driveway too. The trees here don't wait until fall to drop their leaves. Someone is doing it all the time, leaves or flowers, and getting new leaves at the same time.

I have discovered the simple, basic, satisfying grandeur of us being able to make the whole place look loved and cared for at the same time. We are putting all the stuff under the trees in the back to try and change the soil if we can. It must sound a little funny, but I look forward to that part of the day.

I hope you are well. If you need a break from it all you can come and rest in my hammock (it's a proper sleeping one). I just have to watch that the squirrels don't eat the rope. Wait a bit though; it's too hot now. Have you managed to liberate a copy of Ashley's essay? I'm sure that this letter will cross one from you, just wanted to write today, love as always,

Susan

6 May 90

Letter from Mom: meeting Ashley in Singapore is becoming a reality.

Cyclone coming, thunder and lighting.

With this unseasonal cooling, raining, and rewarming, the plants are joyously and profusely confused.

Blows—these are lows to my soul, almost wobbly feeling.

*****

Dear Mom,

THANK YOU. Now I am adjusting to thinking of this whole thing as a reality, not just a dream. Whew. I have just written to Ashley again. This time I said SEE YOU SOON!

Every time I have a doubt, I push it right away.

Oops, the wind is picking up again. There is a cyclone off the coast, apparently heading in. But THEY say that in May they always turn north and don't cross the coast here, but further up. Nearly always. Even if it doesn't hit us, we feel the edges and the air feels a little "adventurous." I am wondering about moving my potted plants from the porch, or around the corner. But I am trying to be casual and to forget about the lightning that hit the tree ten feet from where I was standing the last time a cyclone didn't hit us. At least it's a bit cooler (perhaps low thirties), because of the clouds and delicious moment of rain that waved over just as I was drifting off on my siesta. No, I didn't sleep in the hammock this afternoon.

Everyone here thinks it's a marvellous idea for me to be added in as a helper escort for the group of students when they arrive in Singapore. Already heat- and bug-adjusted. No, time won't drag, except waiting for the postman. I turned over my calendar today, a few days late, but this one shows two months at a time, so it is all spread out right there. May/June. Besides, once I get their information, it will take weeks to deal with tickets and visas. Not visas for there, but to leave and come back here, and to do it all at almost 40°C takes a little longer at every step.

PRIVATE BIT: Just before I received your first letter of extraordinary news (earlier the same day, in fact), I had sent off a last-ditch attempt to see if I could wrench any of the famously lost three thousand dollars. I had been having such dreams and pulls to Ashley and felt so lost not having the possibility to decide freely, just on my own, to come and see him. Then, when I received your missive, I wrote to her again, right away, saying OK NOW. I don't have any real hope, but felt it was worth a shot. I tried to write it without making her feel culpable, and I don't want that to stay in your mind either. Just so you know and also let it go. The thing I really need now is just the schedule. Oh, I wish we could just sit and have tea.

Are you going to put some water lilies so that the kingfishers don't easily get the goldfish? Tell me exactly where the pond is, so that I can picture it. Maybe you can send a little painting just for me with Ashley?

Monday morning, 6:15. After Sunday dinner, partly in the dark, it rained off and on all night, rumbly with thunder still and no electricity. I feel cold. It's confusing at this time of year to feel that. Should I put on jeans? It SOUNDS like November outside, it looks like November, but it's not. It's May in South India and if the sun comes out from behind that cloud for one second with all this water in the air, we will be immediately steam-pressure-cooked. Oh, it will be an interesting day. I will just go to the office.

After breakfast, newspaper weather report, battening the hatches, just in case. Will report.

love, Susan

27 May 90

Is that what happens when you truly give up hoping? It leaves room to live again? I will still try to get to Ashley—do everything I can. I still dream of him, but this country seems to be blocked off—no letters (oh, a few are dribbling through), and for now no phone, or telegrams, or telex.

Last evening, after I had tried for two hours in the morning to call Mom, and realized my attempts were futile and was just numb—too weary inside to feel frustration—with pain in my heart and my throat (full of tears, but they stayed inside—if I let them fall I would be drained to nothing), I started to sweep the garden. I would sweep until I fell asleep. I tried to remember feeling happy; I knew I had felt happy sometimes before. But I didn't fall down and the garden became so beautiful. Then Desiderio came home and "Did I want to cycle to the beach?" "Yes." I could smell the rain coming and feel the rising breeze, and thought yes, surely I can fling myself into that wild mothering saltiness and not come out, just sleep there. But when I stood and looked at the towering waves' roaring power, it was the sea from my dreams that I dream so often. The sleep-times of learning to face them and not be crashed to pulp, to slip under the surface and go through.

31 May 90

CLEARING UP SCRIBBLED PAPERS
Gathering experience to draw from
Making mistakes to learn from

*****

the first-heard drone
    of an airplane
the moment of consciously
    capturing the far-off
    hum
but something musical
    about it
and it's not coming closer
it could be the base
    notes floating here
from a village nighttime
    chanting

CONRAD, JOSEPH

Heart of Darkness

Susan Tait Charman

"Avoid irritation more than exposure to the sun. *Adieu.*"
"In the tropics one must before everything keep calm"...He
lifted a warning forefinger..."Du calme, du calme. *Adieu.*"

Is there something in my letters this summer that inhib-
its a response? If you are in a room with someone and ini-
tiate a conversation and receive no reply, you can fathom
somewhat by the atmosphere if your target is merely preoc-
cupied and didn't hear you, or if they did hear you and are
just taking some time to decide what or if to answer. Then,
in turn, you can decide to stay and wait—or press further—
or leave the room.

*****

I told you that your house was full with the music—not
too full, just full, and that made it hard to walk in. I loved
the music and it was hard to hear it as a shadow from my
house. I was wrong to say it wasn't too loud. I felt like going
for a walk. You were so content and didn't offer me space to
stay. It was all the company you needed, you said.

I withdraw one more pace.

*****

Candlelight—strobes of daylight.
Not the silent distant flashes
But diabolical crashes
Slashing the air

182

Transparent Dreams

Threatening my ear drums

Thunder rolling around them

Pushing the billowing drapes.

House open to catch the cool of the Indian night.

I am no bigger—no more resistant

    Than a drop of the falling rain.

    No more resistant to the stormy pulse

than a drop of

    the falling rain.

*****

I can feel the little

breezes in the air

and I can hear them

I can feel my heartbeats

And against my pillow

I can hear them

But the air is not warm

    or cool

against my skin.

With no shock of coolness

    to define the edges of me

With no covering to know,

    by confining me

The breezes flow through me

My heart beats for it.

12 June 90

By now you must be convinced that your birthday card to John, cheques, and letter are lost—completely. We received it yesterday! One month. Again, thank you. I can almost manage the ticket to Singapore with your gift, and Desiderio will help.

Today I received a fax from Ashley himself. New schedule. Says he had mailed me one but presumes I didn't get it. I didn't, but perhaps it will arrive, maybe with his prize-winning essay inside.

They arrive Singapore on 17 July, and will stay until the 20th. I will go. The itinerary looks perfect to slip into.

I hear your call to come to see you, and am paying attention. This summer is not possible, but I will work on next summer. Forget the winters, unless Hawaii.

Just this moment I finished John's birthday present. I made him a wall hanging (for his ceiling). He had asked if I would someday. It is so seldom he expresses a desire for something. It's a surprise, only from him. Desiderio was delighted, which means that I am content.

I had spoken before about the possibility of joining Janet in her workshop. I have done it—and hired a tailor! There are four of us in the compound, all doing different types of work, but together. THE TAILOR IS MINE! Now I will be able to carry on making individual things like I have been, but NOW just draw the designs, make the patterns, and choose the cloth. I know you were concerned about me wearing myself out. Me too.

Too much news for one aerogram and each thing is really so important to me. I will expand on it all over the next while.

With my love and thank you, S

14 July 90

The dream soon to be real: I leave in two days for Singapore. No one can hold my hand, no one can help me wait. I will go and come alone.

*****

His plane is due. Ashley. I wait again for his arrival as I have for sixteen years. Alone again in a place where there should be someone to hold my hand, to help the waiting. This time, an airport in Singapore. That time before, calling him to be with me, and then his birth. My child.

21 July 90

Golden Landmark Hotel, Singapore

Dear Mom,

Thank you. You have been a support above and beyond the call.

Love Susan

PS: I will type you a long comprehensive report when I get home. It was worth it all. It was important.

Tonight I go back. The kids left yesterday and I am with friends now (new ones, with an Auroville connection) in their home. Out of the hotel! And they have me BUSY, and resting. Both good.

Ashley had written twice. I didn't get them, and also have had no word from you since the one with the cheques. Are you OK? House finished? Painting? Summer guests? My sisters?

Real letter coming,

gratefully, me

5 August 90

Dear Mom,

Suddenly it's been two weeks since I came back from Ashley. A little jet lag, a surprising lot of culture shock for ME (so clean, air-conditioned, full of efficient people, consumerism, electricity that keeps working, nothing green except botanical gardens—strange). Extreme fatigue. A heavy heat wave here, turning into thunderous flooding-everything rain. A little fever. Finding the way back into the (un)routine of my workshop. No Ashley shock though.

He is, of course, much bigger than me now. He says they are moving to a bigger house almost right away, but I have his dad's work address, phone, and fax.

I can't remember now what I told you about him in my note from Singapore, except for thanking you. He is just Ashley, grown into a good young man. I am so pleased with him and for him. He says he wants to come here; "I was born to travel."

I have no idea how many letters in both directions have been lost now. We are all very upset about the mail, not just because of our lack of letters, and beginning to believe that the postman is in the same category as Santa Claus. All of you "out there" aren't in a group that can notice that SOMETHING FUNNY IS GOING ON, but might just think that no one is writing. So now we have started with the Skypak courier again, and have sent our retired higher-up of the Indian Army to Delhi to investigate and straighten things out. There. Now, if you have just been too busy painting and having a nice summer on the island (and I hope you have), please write.

My little workshop seems to be starting off just fine. The small loan I had taken from our Revolving Loan Fund is, of course, almost all used up buying fabric, but that just gets us to the interesting stage.

I have had some pieces in our boutique in Auroville for a few weeks, and they ARE going. We put, just a couple of days ago, the first batch in the Pondy Boutique—more traffic there—and I suddenly have commissions for several wall hangings and room dividers. So if I don't get scared about having to be creative, and just continue on, it looks like everything will be OK. I am not even trying to predict, or speculate, but we are having fun and working hard.

This may seem like a small one to you, but the grocery stall at Bharat Nivas in Auroville now has a deep freeze, and has been buying chicken and fish steaks. I had been DREAMING of protein. I guess the amoebas had depleted all my stored-up power. Now I cook big wonderful fish steaks at least twice a week. Oh, much better. I give them to Desiderio also. Yes, John is eating properly too. I brought back a bunch of almonds from Singapore that I am rationing to myself at lunchtimes.

Give my love to my sisters. I have only one photograph of Ashley and I together in Singapore, so I can't send it away.

Sunday shower time. All the housework is done, even some waxing. I will try the Skypak courier system in the morning. They say twelve to fifteen days for Canada. Let me know.

Always love, me

7 September 90

You know, after a little desolation, this morning, again, the issue of moving had arisen. There was an encouraging moment in the afternoon.

Photographs to be taken for Matrimandir project

1. doorways and entrances
2. ladders and steps (overexpose)
3. reflection
4. small children
5. inner chamber (model)
6. centre top from the roof
7. John's travel from camp
8. space frame, close up to node, sky background, dissolve flowers.
9. night-twilight
10. Models, library, spiral, and MM Nursery (one roll)
11. doves
12. MM from underneath
13. sunrises and sunsets
14. looking up inside sphere of Matrimandir
15. Mother's and Sri Aurobindo's symbols
16. banyan tree and flowering trees in the gardens
17. the Chamber, with the crystal globe and without.

Hibiscus Nursery Photographs

Beauty of Supramental Love (flower of Auroville)

Beauty of Supramental Youth (single, salmon with pale yellow reddish streaks)

Progress (white, red streaks)

Psychic Power in Existence (small single, intense magenta)

Ananda (small single delicate, slightly crinkled, cream)

Light (white)

Aesthetic Power of Beauty (single, reddish pink)

Power of Supramental Consciousness (double yellow, white heart)

Integral Wealth of Mahalaxmi (water lily)

Richness of Feelings (easter lily cactus, pink)

Psychological Perfection (varieties)

8 October 90

Found a new pen.

Can this work for a left-handed soul?

Maybe.

Exercise For A Left-handed Person

exercise for the eyes.

realized it's a whole different

I just read this over and

to not smear the whole thing?

at the bottom of the page

climate, it's sensible to start writing

person, don't you think, especially in this

Now, for a left-handed

PART TWO
1990

I had never wanted a workshop, a business, but suddenly my dreams were too big to materialize alone. I needed help.

The surrounding compounds, the creative groups in Auroville, mostly (admirably) hire women from the local villages. I didn't.

The boys had skills I needed. Thinking back, I felt that if I could give the men challenging work with dignity and pride, and they could carry that feeling home with them, it would spread.

And they could help me build my place. It was simple. Six granite pillars, a keet roof, a cement floor. Two sewing machines, a little handwoven cotton, and we began.

From the beginning, the work we did was complex and meticulous. The designs grew and techniques developed from my years and years of quilting. Now, faced with the magic of Indian fabrics, the madness of colour and light, dreams flew.

I didn't speak Tamil; they didn't speak English (very much). So we worked together. I watched endlessly how they worked, adding their skills to mine. When our abilities were combined, achieving the impossible became possible.

I made huge line drawings and turned them into puzzle pieces; they were cut apart, colours chosen for each piece, and reassembled with fine French seams. Larger and larger, more intricate as time passed. I worked at pulling the images from my visions onto paper and then to floating panels, streaming with light, multiple layers changing mood with the turning of the day.

I pushed myself and pulled them with me. We brought a third tailor in. We worked with an unsustainable level of concentration and occasionally cracked under it. They took advantage of me. We learned to take breaks; brain holidays, I called them.

Very quickly, from the start even, attention gathered to my dream. To our little group. The work sold. I could carry on. There was always just enough money to pay my people, to buy cloth. But not always for me. I grew thinner.

I would compromise by creating things I loved that people were happy to buy, but not compromise myself by losing the dream in cold business. For me it would have amounted to prostitution.

My original tailor left. His ambitions were different.

Siva stayed. The shine in his eyes was a joy each morning. From the beginning I loved to see his sparkle. He made me furious. He was brilliant, incorrigible and mischievous. I fired him. I took him back. I fired him again, and he quit all in a burst.

He was gone. I didn't hear. No one told me where he was. For weeks. One morning, early, there he was, standing, lost-looking, with an open gaze into my heart. With a huge white bandage round his head.

A freak and probably karmic accident had befallen. Picture the boy on his moped, making the trip to Pondicherry down the tree-lined quiet back road. Passed by a van with a ladder on the roof, under a too-low branch. The ladder swept off onto Siva's head. Stitches, concussion, in bed for weeks. And no one told me.

Not a story even he could make up.

"I can start on Monday?" a question-lilted statement I couldn't and didn't want to refuse.

A new level was reached, and the visions expanded and exploded into exhibitions. The Alliance Française in Pondicherry asked me to show. We made a spectacle of the cavernous halls. Thousands of metres of floating panels stirred by the slow swirl of fans, lit and moody with colour.

1 September 90

Dear Mom,

Happy Birthday yesterday!

John and I were thinking to phone you, but it would have been the middle of your night when we could have managed it, and therefore more shocking than funny.

I persuaded him (and me) to take a whole day off and go with a boatload of people looking for dolphins. Yes, they found us, and we all went swimming out at sea, and all have tropical sunburns (except our noses, thanks to some Strength 25 Super Sunstop that I put on everyone. I can't remember just who left that particular brand behind, but twenty-one of us are grateful.

All is well, busy. John received your letter, haven't seen photos yet. A proper letter will come to you after I get the one you were writing on your return trip on the ferry.

This one is just Happy Birthday, with my love, always,

Susan

31 October 90

Dear Mom,

Thank you. At last a letter. I can't remember how up to date I have you. I know I wrote at least a couple of times since seeing Ashley in Singapore.

You've caught me in a day of dilemma.

The workshop: I have been making beautiful things with my little gang for the past while, with my tailor, mostly hangings for windows and doorways. We had huge fun materializing the window panels for the conference-type space of the new Guest House. Windows on three sides of the room needed eight panels, each five by six feet. It's one continuous landscape, starting with sunrise (on the side where the sun comes up), ocean and low hills, and gradually changes terrain and time of day (and therefore colour) around to the third wall and the moon, with purpley hills and sand dunes. They are done, finished and paid for, but the building isn't ready.

We have three more for other rooms, complete up to the border finishing because the doors and windows aren't in yet and they have curved tops, so must be fitted carefully—and she can't pay me. I will finish them anyway; they are so close to being done. And then we can carry on with other things.

Also, my "master embroiderer" is there. I haven't had him as long as my tailor (photos included)—really, his work is unimaginable, and all the pieces until this last have been requested or sold before they were off the frame. But that also means that no one (hardly) has seen them, or even knows that we are doing that kind of work. So, we have just managed to do a huge (about fifty-by-one-hundred-inch) black Kashmiri wool shawl with a full border of flowers and leaves on a vine and a wonderful dragon (not scary), with incredible colours and work, about four or five feet long in the middle. I will put him in the Pondy Boutique.

But all these things take time to make and we need silk thread and on and on. So far I've been managing without falling into the trap of a production line. It makes me almost fall into tears at the thought of that, and every cell in my body rebels.

But because we are a new unit with nothing to fall back on, it's not easy. I may have to let Velu (the embroiderer) and his son go for a while and have them do contract work from home. But then I can't so easily decide with him each colour as we go on with a design. I don't know. Today I know nothing; I feel.

This is not crying on your shoulder. I just want you to know what I am doing, what I am trying. Exploring this creativity, <u>working</u> at it, seems to be the only thing that halfway satisfies me, or makes me feel I'm on the right track.

Come and sit with us and paint, Mom. You might feel too lazy, but the rest of those things you said aren't true. You are healthy and not old and you may be carrying more pounds than you think you want, but you just look comfortable and good. Nobody here remembers you as a fat person. And Desiderio says you don't have to speak French, and I said "but Helen didn't understand a word you said," and he said, "I don't speak much anyway." That's true.

And we can get around the bicycle thing.

This all was talked over at breakfast when I reported your letter, and once again you saying, "You come," I think about getting John and I there. I don't know if it's humanly possible for me to raise that kind of money. Not at this stage, anyway, it isn't. It will take several years, but it IS a goal. Desiderio says that I can't send John alone because he would run out of things to say after five minutes. That's true too.

I would dearly love Desiderio also to see the wide spaces of Canada. Who would hold the fort here? That's a dream.

Somewhere in the last page it became the next day (Nov 1).

The villagers are saying that we are on day fifteen of a forty-day rain. Often they are right about those things. We are soggy and have the odd sniffle, but I think in the villages it is more than miserable. Leaking keet roofs and crumbling walls, just wet wet wet where they sleep and everywhere else too, the whole time, and cold.

Today it's 24°C, but it's grey and windy, and soaking wet. I don't have a waterproof raincoat, but can come home and change and put on something dry(ish) and get warm. They can't.

Today I was given, not a loan, but an advance against the sale of the dragon! That means that I can buy enough cloth to keep us going for awhile, and lets me breathe. It will be OK.

And someone left two presents at my door while I was out. Even wrapped. One is a very unusually (interestingly) cut white skirt and the other a traditional caftan. Long-sleeved, white on white jacquard-weave cotton, beautifully soft with golden-beige embroidery on the sleeves and all around the neck and front opening.

And my young friend Akash brought me some chicken: "It was too much for him and Barbara."

There is much to be grateful for. I shall carry on.

It didn't rain for two days now. Madras has had its full season quota in one week.

I want to know how you really are, and who is the "we" in your "not deciding about the winter yet"? Is it Viola being a good friend? Sounds like neighbours are there. I'm glad. Give my love to them all, hugs to you and my sisters.

9 December 90

Dear Mom,

You must have received my longish letter just after you mailed your card. I hope so, cause I went on for days!

Thanks, Mom. I hadn't expected a cheque at all, but it was very welcome—and timely.

It seems, just since the last few weeks, that at last I will be able to manage the workshop without being pulled into what I dreaded most: a production line. At this moment I have work lined up that will take us through to the end of February. Whew!

This should have been posted in Vancouver by a visitor to Auroville who will be there for a week on his way to Saskatchewan. I will load him with letters and arm him with phone numbers so he can reassure everyone that we are alive and well. (He's not someone I ever see except to pass on the road, but he is a "nice Canadian young man" and some direct contact is kind of fun.)

I will write better after the end of the week when this big Guest House deadline is over and my tailor goes away for eight days on a pilgrimage, and I (theoretically) have some time at home. Really it's a blessing that I have some clear time to make all the drawings without him sewing furiously behind my every step.

And HOW ARE YOU?

love, Susan

PS: Here's an article about my workshop for you, from the December issue of our *Auroville Today* newspaper, written by Tineke.

"I Like To Create Things For People"

To express themselves, some people use their body, others play an instrument or use clay or pencil and paintbrush. But for Susan the medium is cloth. With simple handloom cotton she creates kaftans, hangings and bedcovers, each one of them a real piece of art.

She has always worked with fabric, no matter what else she was doing in Canada, where she used to live. When she arrived in Auroville, four years ago, she began taking up jobs, while continuing her fabric designs as a sideline. But then she understood that this was where her heart really was, and she decided to dive into it fully. What started out as a one-woman enterprise has now expanded. "I needed help, so I decided to hire a tailor. I was fortunate enough to find one who can understand what I want and put together my puzzles of cloth. Then he brought me a master embroiderer, whom I did not need, but...I could not afford *not* to take him! I got a loan to buy materials, we built this small workplace—and now I have a business. I am not a businesswoman, but I need this umbrella above me (I am part of Janet's Joy workshop) so that I can explore the feelings I want to express in cloth."

It is a joy to walk into Susan's workshop and to see the tailor create intricate hangings out of all these coloured pieces of cotton. Or watch the embroiderer and his son transform plain wool into shawls with dragons, or waistcoats with lotus flowers or fishes. "We all work closely together. I give some ideas and then I leave him free to use his craft and skill. If he does not get this freedom to play, this craft of rural India will be lost." Each piece which gets produced is unique. "Sometimes people ask me if I want to make several pieces of the same design. Or whether I plan to go into mass production in order to have a successful workshop. But this makes every cell in me rebel. To repeat things makes it too boring for me. I like to create things for people. This direct contact is very satisfying for me—but I don't take orders!"

7 February 91

Dear Mom,

Wednesday morning. Today is a strike—not quite ALL India, but enough so that those of us with workshops are quietly home. Workers will be harassed in their villages if they attempt to go to work. It is really lovely and quiet. It's okay for garden watchmen, etc. to come to work, so our two are here. The watering is getting done. Desiderio has gone to Matrimandir, also John. They will also have a quiet day.

This houseful has postponed a bit my letter writing. Desiderio's mother has arrived without incident, but I don't know about their return being so easy. We are trying not to speculate. When I tried to confirm their return flight the other day, the agent said to wait because all the schedules are changing. The WAR, of course, is affecting comings and goings here. I have met people who just arrived from Paris on a tour nine days late because all the airplanes (not all) are being conscripted for the Gulf, heard of others from Holland being stuck for days on end in Karachi, others routed through Sri Lanka (who are not here yet).

But yes, our people who were stuck in Kuwait are back safely. They had been very fortunate; the woman and little children were among the first to be released. The husband was kept for a longer time but is good. I saw him briefly, and he said that the experience of those who had been living in the East was a help in coping with the strange situation of waiting, of not knowing, of being calm in a uneasy time.

I'm not sure if anyone is getting a clear picture of what is going on in the Gulf, but here the information we are fed is obviously distorted. A mixture of the Hindu daily newspaper and the BBC radio. But on the other hand, the effects on our daily lives feel so direct. There will be changes, I'm sure. But what? Mostly it feels like an important time to keep contacts, not to worry just for the sake of worrying, and to trust somehow that this is all a chance for a beginning of some new way of being together on the earth, not only a mad disaster.

What winter we were having seems to be over. Already. We wore our socks at night for about six times in January. Sweaters for a few days.

Two days ago I started out in the morning for Pondy for a day on my own with a completely esoteric list in my pocket. My vague plan was to begin on foot and pick a ride, normally no problem at all. But I left a bit too early, got a ride for about a mile in the middle, still in Auroville, and WALKED, and walked and walked. I looked in all the fabric shops and found some beautifully smooth handloom light cotton, came home with three gigantic dahlias grown in the Ashram garden, an armload, and a clay elephant for the garden.

I did succumb to taking a taxi home after being there the entire day. One has to say, casually, "Just take me home; how much is it? Can I pay now?" "Certainly, madam." And then slip in, "Now I have done everything; we just must pick up a few parcels here and there." Six big bags left at the Aristo hotel; the car was half-full already after that, and then the flowers that I had left in a cool shop, and then, "Oh, just the elephant." We had to tilt him to get his head in the door, and not to break the trunk. "No! He isn't heavy; he weighs less than me!" (just).

Today I am almost recovered from my sunstroke. After a bit I will go and wash a pile of the cloth so my tailors will have something to play with. I have taken on another one. Partly because the projects we are doing are becoming more and more intricate, that it is heavy going for Dhaya. He can do it all, but I don't want to burn him out, or me. And also because it has snuck up on me that we have so many projects lined up that we don't even have time to think about doing anything for the boutiques. I am extremely fortunate to have had Dhaya find Siva, who also speaks English (and can read my handwriting even upside down—I know even right-side up takes a knack), and is also a beautiful sweet young man. They both have a real shine somehow.

Now, when I have to go off and look at houses with a client, or sit by myself to draw or think (thinking usually means working in the garden or writing to one's mother, etc.) until some picture filters down, I don't feel badly about leaving only one man to work there all by himself, getting bogged down. He is in charge of working out how they share the work.

Okay, the cloth is done. Mercifully for me, there was a little white cloud shading me from the sun, and only about twenty-five metres of stuff. With this handloom cloth, the colours are wonderful, but every one metre they daub SOMETHING on to mark it. It does scrub out pretty easily, but you've got to do it.

Just glanced at the thermometer. In here under the trees, it is a very pleasant, breezy twenty-seven, no sweat—but out in the sun it's a bit strong.

Oh, it's only the beginning of February. John and I and everyone else had a wistful thought of snow on Pender Island. Yes, I know it's a little different when it is cold and raining. Maybe candles are the business to go into.

I'm glad everyone was there with you over the holiday season. We agree that it's probably a good thing for the girls to preserve their relationship by seeing each other without their men. You don't let everybody read your letters, do you?

Rest—lunch—back to you.

I woke up from my rest wondering what you are painting. Also remembering the day when I was with you and Dad on the island, and you went off to your pottery studio and I to sew one morning, and we each had decided to write and draw with our other hands, only discovering it at lunchtime. And I am wondering now if we are on similar self-exploratory tracks without knowing.

Now is time for the plumeria to really bloom. And I picked some cosmos yesterday at a friend's house. Took a pocketful of seeds and scattered them a bit when I got home. Beside all the rest of these flamboyant, exotic blooms, I find them oddly touching. I suppose because they are familiar from forever. Just little fragile wild things.

Suddenly we have swooped through to just before dinner the next day. It's made. It's salad. We are all clean. I am not going to do one single thing more today, too sleepy, but okay...

to be continued, with my love,

Susan

PS: The little red seeds that I sent along to you are from a tree in the garden. They will last for a very long time just as they are and I think surely you can string them. If they wear out, we have LOTS. The shell is from the beach, and the seedpod too; it has floated from very far away, from Africa, Desiderio says. These are the best presents we can do on such short notice and with him having "only one foot" these days (the foot will recover).

xoxoxox

Susan and Desiderio

8 February 91

PPS: Please can you send your recipe for hermits and do you have one for sponge cake that has orange or lemon juice?

Ginger snaps?

Icebox cookies? You know the ones you used to put in the fridge in wax paper?

Gingerbread?

Date nut loaf?

Peanut butter cookies?

With love,

Susan and Janet

Some afternoons we just feel like sneaking out of the workshop into her kitchen. It's good for us.

11 March 91

I was just getting into bed and looked in the mirror. I am sure that I am much less tanned now. Most of me is NEVER exposed to the sun except for doing the laundry and then I'm in the shade. Never mind skin cancer, it's also not amusing to deal with liver, kidneys, and general sunstroke if one is forced by circumstance to spend unwise time in the sun.

I really don't mind the heat, but the sun is hard. There. Relax.

Sunday afternoon and the laundry's done. Now it's just after three. I have decided today it would be a bit fanatical to finish cleaning before about four. Suddenly, again, it's too hot too soon. No one is quite ready for summer; here it seems bigger than life.

Between more absorbing projects in the workshop we are making hats. So many people have asked. Nice, big-brimmed, pretty colours. It always makes me think of you saying "WEAR A HAT!" OK, Mom.

An American friend was just here, and took many pictures in the workshop. I asked her to please send copies to you.

I don't know how I look on film just now. But if you think I'm too thin, try not to worry. I am healthy. Some weeks I have a small chicken with John and then again share one with someone else.

Work progresses. Although I think my drawing is improving, it's most a question of seeing clearly. You know this. Even if a design comes from a picture in my mind, a feeling is starting to come of being able to hold it still long enough to look closely and make a sketch. Something is happening and I'm trying to stay in the right place to let it. So far, I need cloth to "do it," but that can change.

We are all working pretty hard, so anyone who comes must be ready to "make their own experience," as the saying goes—but seeing as how I am the boss in my workshop, my days can be pretty flexible.

The floor is washed. Just as I was getting up to do that I thought of something I wanted to say, and then realized with a jolt that there's a whole side of my life I've been leaving out. Unwittingly.

I will try to make it more complete now.

Oh, no need to hold your breath.

Now it's the next day—because I really was thinking about it.

Most of what is hard to put on paper is the inner work. Inner work is probably the best phrase, rather than something like "spiritual," which always tends to sound religious, or flat.

Maybe a LIST is the thing.

EQUANIMITY: I like that word, and say it often to myself. I think you have had much more of it than I. My best example of progress in this area occurred one night when the current was out and I was leaving Desiderio with the FULL milk tin in my hand. I stepped out the door in the dark and a frog jumped on my face and stuck there and slowly slid down. Imagine it, pitch-dark. I thought it was at least a snake. I barely screamed and DID NOT spill the milk.

PATIENCE

PLASTICITY...no, a list isn't the way.

24 March 91

May is the hottest but March is the hardest month. We are not ready, never ready for this oppression. We cling to shreds of sanity. We try to remember, remind each other, that NOTHING can crack or destroy our souls, not heat or amoebas.

We ride out these waves of transition into full-blown Indian summer when we can float more gently in pools of sweat and mild fever.

God. March. We try not to panic in the rising temperature. Some comfort in not taking it too personally. We fight it together, trying to keep our tempers and emotions cool. I dream of sailing.

And I am now awakened by the intrusion of the dropping of dew from fog-obscured predawn air. It falls on the deepening earth cover of sun-scorched almond and eucalyptus leaves with a force more than one would deem possible, for dew. Wrung from the sky by the push of the sun still beyond the horizon. I stay contentedly awake. The best moments of the day: the brief morning sea breeze.

Sunday morning, hard red earth swept smooth. Cool elegant shadow of the royal palm. I stop in it. A sophisticated calm place. Still, or sways as a whole. And the plumeria shade shimmers. The air there is a tepid bath with fragrant frangipani oils.

Giardia medicine Saturday evening. Still shaky in the morning. A clear day.

Monday
25 March 91

Giardia medicine again last night.

In the a.m., shaky, swollen glands later (neck, groin, breasts), but OK, not crazy.

27 March 91

Woke busy with ideas.

29 March 91

Big gap, I know; I got feeling a bit "not well" but am OK now. It's always hard to tell in this season, when the heat starts to settle in, if it's "just the heat" or a menopausal moment—or WHAT. But this is the time for parasites (amoebas, etc.). I took the medicine last weekend. I think they are gone.

30 March 91

I will go in May to housesit in another community. A little distance is needed.

31 March 91

Did I need that much of a bonding, that much of a safe home so I wouldn't fly off until I could be ready to make my own place here, that I was taken in by someone so charismatic right at the beginning?

It's nearly confirmed that I will housesit for friends during May and June. This proximity of living is not easy—not living with Desiderio, nor separately. It's not like neighbours, so I can't just think it's like that, and I don't particularly want to move away, but I feel I must take a break and see what to do. The more evolved our relationship becomes, the closer we are, really. But I need to see from a little distance; Auroville from a different angle. No drama—it feels right to do this at this moment because it keeps arising again and again. It's good for me to find out that there ARE possibilities open to me, after all this time of being so protected here, and I wonder if I don't worry sometimes about having a home of my "own" or even coming to visit you, because I think that I CANNOT.

I will be here still for another month. It will be interesting, partly because to have a conversation with someone you love dearly that went, "I don't know what to do, I keep doing stupid things; I am afraid of hurting us. I think I should housesit for a couple of months and step out of YOUR very strong atmosphere, and see what MINE feels like. Maybe you'll be relieved I'm gone and maybe you'll miss my presence, and maybe I'll go out there and find I was at home after all."

And from him: "I don't know what to do either; you can't hurt US. You need a break from me, let's try."

Just to be able to have a conversation of that sort is a clearing in itself and a release of tension, and it is even with a small feeling of excitement and happiness that I can feel free to make a small trial wing-spreading flight from my safe nest here. A little adventure.

It's only seven minutes by bicycle from here, so I can still come for breakfast if I want. You see, really no drama, but important somehow. NOTE: After going back to number the pages, aha! That's the trouble with writing over a period of weeks: one appears to contradict oneself:

"I don't mind the heat."

"It's too hot."

"I am healthy."

"I have giardia."

"I am fine now."

All true in their time. Everything passes.

John is well too. I made him a hat. He always wears one, but some are pretty dreadful. This one looks like Indiana Jones.

Is that a new speed bump stretching across the path? It's just out of focus range of my eyeglasses. Slow the bicycle. Stop the bicycle. Oops. Wait. It's a very big long fat snake, sneaking back into the jungle. I don't know what kind of snake it is. It's a big snake. I wait for his tail to finish crossing before I go past.

Send more photos. love,

Susan

3 April 91 (night)

Heat-fatigued weight
  of my body
pressed so hard against
  the mattress—bruising
  heaviness
can't move.
Night fog glinting
moonlight flashes
from the slow movement
of dew-laden leaves,
swaying, as it slides
  down
    no breeze.

24 April 91

Dear Mom,

Just this moment I got your letter, and will pass it to John at dinner tonight.

We, here, cringe at the thought of you moving into the city. John thought it a possibility to consider—eventually—presuming compatibility, an amalgamation of houses with a friend? Maybe you could share taking care of one house, chores, companionship? I liked that idea also. I feel, too, that you treasure your independence.

It IS warm enough here. Nearly time to get serious about summer clothes. Nighttime minimum about 28°C, daytime around 35° or so. Do I say that every time? It's always true.

I am not housesitting yet, but the feeling of it is getting to be more of a gentle spreading out than a shift.

I am supposed to be drawing. Dhaya is giving me space to do that calmly by taking a couple of days to put on borders and line the eight panels that are ready so far in this project.

A whole new roof? What a nuisance. I have to get a new door frame for my front (only) door. Termites. In this place, THAT is a production.

to be continued, hello to everyone you can think of,

with love always, Susan

A Reminder: Equanimity

Written on a chocolate bar wrapper

What kind of test of equanimity is this for me? Am I to watch you fall, and feel that your friend has gone away? He wasn't—I had only felt that, but a week later he IS gone from here. We adjust the milk and curd without a word. I just do it. You say he isn't gone, but he is not here, when he comes back, do I just readjust the milk and curd without a word, and not remember your tears? Me, who is not your companion, but who lives here with you.

Help me not to fall after I have held you with my heart through the depths and now that you have the strength to manage again I am left empty, in a way, from the space that your need filled up. You didn't ask for help or holding; I guess you are just waiting.

11 May 91

Yesterday evening I had a vision of your face. Strong and beautiful and clean, and sad inside. And you shook your head—no—at me. No words, just a feeling of "please, not yet."

How can I call for help? I am so surely out of place I don't know if I can stand it. And how can I go back?

This is beyond sadness; this is grief. I am afraid I've gone too far. I am afraid.

12 May 91

I did call. He did come.

Everything had become too big at the same time. Back in proportion. He was also reassuring. It is worth it for us to take this time, and he will also take me to dinner next week, after his fever.

What I see here this morning is that I have my drawing outside taking up the entire porch, but the house is clean. There is music if I want, and cold things in the fridge.

In my own home, I am missing: the opportunity for the domesticity that contents me, the room to wander a bit, and company.

When all those things are so close but withheld, I feel a deprivation. Now let's just carry on, and see.

After lunch: there's no harm in folding up the drawing for the enormous commission I'm doing for a few days. It's not good to work on something for someone else when I am so in need of rest, and even a little exercise. Maybe later I will try something smaller, less cumbersome and over-whelming. There is time.

John is coming for chicken soup.

Nice time with him. He wished only for chamomile tea, and I had some.

Monday, 13 May 91

Morning, tea, shower—now what?

Don't cry.

Made it to my workshop. Not OK. Boys were not there. Went to check my house, sweep and water. Fine and quiet. Passed by the workshop long enough to say that if my boys come now they should go home again.

Sleep, eat, garden. Have I been attempting too much all at once? I have decided for this moment to let myself off the hook for anything that is not essential. Even the pressure of work—of creating.

It's hot today. I walk into the house, stripping off clothes as I go, aiming for the open-walled bathroom and the bucket shower.

Damn. There's a big snake coming in over the low wall. I stop. He stops. What to do? Be calm. What will he do if he's panicked by the smooth, waxed floor? I see, finally, that there's a big frog head-first halfway into his mouth. Ah. He can't bite me, he's already occupied.

I shall forgo the shower for now.

I go to the low daybed and take a nap. He will be gone when I wake up. I hope.

14 May 91

Morning. Started happy when I woke. Feel some strength of my own. I smiled, and shut my workshop for the rest of the week. I can't work.

I feel a violent welling up of something—fear?

I am whole, perfect, strong, powerful, creative, loving, and happy.

I am whole, perfect, strong, powerful, creative, loving and happy.

I am whole, perfect, strong, powerful, creative, loving, and happy.

I need five thousand dollars. Soon.

I wrote one last letter to the woman who owes me money and burned it.

Ohm.

Wednesday, 15 May

Perhaps if I try my mother's adage: just accomplish one thing today.

16 May 91

Slipping. I can smile on the surface, I can talk, eat, this morning I could draw.

Not now.

I want out (right now I feel that way).

How do I find again the strength I felt yesterday morning?

I would like the friends I'm housesitting for to come home now.

Saturday a.m.

Exercises last evening helped.

J'essaie a reste calme. J'essaie qu'est que tu dit chaque jour.

Je pense que je ne peux pas reviens sans d'être moins de la tristesse, plus du calme, de la force. Je veux seulement le mieux que je peux, et à porter seulement les bonnes choses a toi.

20 May 91

Remember the sailing, remember the setting off, the adventure of each moment. No expectations. No possible speculation; the journey is the thing.

I had nothing but enough money for my fare and the clothes in my pack. The warm winter sailing things sent back by post when the part of the journey where I needed them was done. To make my bag lighter still.

21 May 91

RAJIV GHANDI ASSASSINATED

The assassination of Rajiv Ghandi, the ex-prime-minister of India, occurred as a result of a suicide bombing in Sriperumbudur, near Chennai, in Tamil Nadu on 21 May 1991. At least fourteen others were also killed.

Thursday
23 May

OHM

We gave up working in the middle of the day. Uneasy gangs of thugs happy for trouble.

Friday
24 May

OHM

Work—will the boys come?

Food—will the shops be open?

I have a piece of bread. I will save it for tonight.

Fruit I can find and milk will come.

*****

Why do I feel, in the larger scheme of things, that it is necessary for me to be there with you?

No work again.

We are all running out of food a bit. Kidneys feel a strain from making do. Tomorrow maybe we can all get the food we need.

The funeral was today.

Where do I start to write my book? At teatime this morning at the Guest House, my friend Silvano said, "You should WRITE, Susan. Write a book. Start in the middle."

This age of forty-two, where I am, this brink of full womanhood on a graph, on a lifeline, may be a middle. But it's a beginning. Shifting. Not shiftless, but adjustments to refine and make true my course.

Friday night

Caterpillar attack.

LOST the next day.

Ohm

Sunday

I do feel welcome when you hold me, even briefly. This morning I didn't realize how much of a gap that fills until I had to walk away without it.

Perhaps there can be no sign from you until after I have made my statements. Or are they there and I haven't listened closely enough?

Pearls get beautiful and lustrous by living gracefully in an uncomfortable situation.

I don't believe you. Your declarations of non-attachment. I believe you aspire for that but that your apparent coldness and the aggressively defensive air you create would NOT BE

THERE if you were doing it in a way that felt truly correct to yourself.

In the corner of my life that includes you, there are no boundaries. I wish for endless patience and goodwill.

I have just yelled in my head at you for two hours or more, and now I see, again, that you are far more steadfast that I could have hoped for.

Harmony.

This is all so extraordinarily simple, yet my mind is raising every doubt, every resistance possible. Let them come, let them go.

28 May 91

Fourth day ginseng—good.

1 June 91

Head bonking in the kitchen, then sick sick sick. Which came first: the chicken or the head egg? Days lost again, but, surprisingly, workshop goes on.

Ohm

Wednesday
5 June

My only enemies are fear and doubt.

I AM worthy of my place. It is every atom's right to be in their place.

11 June 91

Slipping since yesterday. I can feel the same despair trying to come. I did all the right things.

Wednesday

Still no current—sleepy, lazy-feeling, quiet.

14 June 91

This weather, this before-the-rain, the pulsing pressure of it, pushes me near to tears, pulls me to want to be held like a child.

I need it to rain.

At 5:00 p.m. a Payne's-grey sky, and beneath everything is shining golden in anticipation of the storm. I can hear the sea from here, roaring, pushing against the land, a breeze so slight that only the lightest of leaves move, and a soothing coolness touches my forehead.

But I think it is a false promise of relief. The moisture will not actually fall, but rest suspended in oppressive night, held till morning, and steamed into clouds at dawn.

Ah, the current is back. Pray it stays. It's not been very steady at all.

Rabowka is curled on my lap. I think we both want to feel cozy.

CATS:

RABOWKA (mother)

BINGO

MONSTER (green eyes)

ALABASTER (cross-eyed white one)

Saturday
15 June 91

Election Day

Dawning of Election Day. Holiday. See nothing, no one, but know that the army is surrounding us, keeping a lid on. I suppose we will hear stories from outside this bubble later.

It poured torrentially in the night. There is, of course, an aftermath. Don't look yet, it's still too dark anyway to start cleaning. Pot of tea, blinders on, feet up with my book till seven. The roof didn't leak, but the rain misted sideways into your room downstairs. I had protected your bed there before I slept and it didn't reach your desk. I polished off the moisture.

Bingo threw up on the floor in the kitchen; he has worms. He's out looking for grass now. Then the ants came.

Everything is scrubbed and disinfected now, even all evidence of toads is gone for the moment. But I am not hungry anymore, and I don't want to feed the cats this morning. I want them to go hunting for toads and the thing in the cupboard that I say is a shrew (but it's quite big). There's a frog in the toilet, but if I put enough water in a big splash he will go down and stay. Do they plug the drain?

Cinnamon toast—maybe I can eat that.

16 June 91

Why so hard, the thunder and lightning? I try to relax through it.

Ohm

17 June 91

I am whole, perfect, strong, powerful, creative, loving, and happy.
I am whole perfect strong powerful creative loving and happy.
I am whole perfect strong powerful creative loving and happy...

Self-expression: the need for it. Can I channel it all into my work, my friendships, perhaps an ongoing writing, and be able to live quietly and happily, grateful for a quiet place?

Don't take this depression personally. I am not that.

21 June 91

Basics only today.

Workshop: the project of the moment is a seascape, two by twenty-six metres long (approximately the proportions of a twelve-inch ruler). Thirteen panels around three sides of a room (mostly windows). The request is for the subject matter to be the ocean—no storms, no animals. I've worked out a design that begins at sunset on one panel around the corner into the hallway, continuing on through evening and night with sunrise occurring on the panels that coincide with the natural morning. The drawing carries through to late afternoon at the far end of the last wall. The colours morph, and waves and sky change subtly as it goes along. Handloom cotton. French seams. Wow. Can you imagine how much newspaper had to be glued together to make the original drawing on? And then when that becomes the pattern with designated colours for each puzzle piece, there is another set of panels to place below those sheets. Those will remain intact, with numbers and colours designating each portion. I keep all those, nicely folded into large brown envelopes, identified and filed away for reference. Those boys, young men, of mine are so special.

Wednesday
26 June 91 I think (yes)

What is that sound? A percussion band? A lorry of part-emptied oil drums on the dirt road? Something interesting. It's getting louder, or closer, or both. It's a pleasing, plunking, happy NOISE. A jazz band in the peanut field? Coconuts bouncing off a high tile roof? It's gone now—but the frogs keep on.

Cycled home though the high-humidity air, an underwater glaze on my eyes. Push down the hill against the uphill breeze. Slowly drifting through the pristine rhythm of newly furrowed fields.

2 July 91 (1–2 night)

Dream of a prayer

Wrote it to put in the box in the library. Worried that the words weren't right. The committee would recognize my handwriting and perhaps be judging me. Decided it didn't matter. If I was sincere, that's all that mattered.

4 July 91

I felt truly that I had at last found a home where I was welcome. A place to work from, inside and out. Where I could learn to be quiet, and there was room to share some of the joyful parts and some of the hard parts.

Now I must weigh whether things need sharing, and if they are urgent. And if they do feel urgent, that makes a risk of involvement that you don't want. So I only tell you mostly light things, which probably seem frivolous, but it's only a need for some measure of sharing.

I'm dreaming it; I can't stop dreaming it. Can I shift inside somehow to make it easy?

I don't know how to continue. I must, but I don't know how.

Later morning: I begin to realize the pressure I put on myself, expecting to have all my weaknesses taken care of while housesitting—to go back cheerful, strong, resolved, independent, needing no one.

Neatly and cleanly make the step to a new stage of maturity in a crash course like summer school. Final exam upon return to my house. "What have I learned in my summer vacation?" The essay to be presented and graded, but not commented upon.

Saturday
20 July 91

The last two weeks, those dreams were true. Suddenly it's easy. Simply not interesting any more. Even small left-over shards of anger or pique drop away.

Letter from Ashley—my son—that's all. He slips in like he was never away from me.

12 August 91

Dear Mom,

You are getting close to me sending you some International Reply Coupons like we used to send to John! I haven't heard from you for so long. And I even had a letter from Ashley the other day!

I remember answering your letter that said, "You come," and perhaps my reply sounded cool, or harsh; it was NOT meant that way AT ALL, and perhaps because I feel more settled recently, I am beginning to think more easily of a visit. I know it's important. I do miss you, that was never in question. Do you understand what I am trying to say? Perhaps it's that this place is not easy, but it feels like my place (I didn't ask for easy). If I had come, or planned to come, during a time when, for instance, my work wasn't so established (in its funny way), or before I had made certain decisions in my life, it would have been a case of running home. It wouldn't have made you happy either.

Let me work on finding a way to bring <u>us</u> there. John and I have already spent several delightful dinners making plots. So something must be in the offing, for it to be coming up so often.

Even though it's busy summertime for you, send me an update. I need to know how you are. I get concerned, and I have a worry that I have hurt your feelings, and that is not OK with me.

always, Susan

YELLOW COIL NOTEBOOK

15 September 91

My dearest friend,

Now I can write—or begin.

Sunday afternoon

I've been trying to talk to you for months. Probably a good thing that the time slipped by and the waves went over, without my reporting it all blow by blow.

Except for my letter of affirmation of being "whole, perfect, etc.," that helped a lot. I hope it didn't worry you.

Are you there? Are you all right?

Did you get my letter that said I will try to come next year?

22 September 91

Dear John,

So funny having you be in Bombay, while I've been away from my home too.

My housesitting episode is over. Weekend break at Centre Guest House in between.

It seems clear now that all the trauma at the beginning of that little side journey was because it is a time for real changes, real letting go. I was glad for your being near. Then I know you saw me becoming more myself. I want you to know I am happy.

Like starting again. It's almost five years since I came to this house. Now, if I choose, it is my home.

love, your akka (older sister)

*****

Some hard dreams this week. One of a man with no arms or legs, trying to get me. He was in a hole completely covered with dirt, trying to get out and couldn't. I saw, inside the dream, that even if he managed to get out, he had no power to hurt me.

21/22 September 91

Last night dream

In a circle with several men (exercises?). Suddenly, as I was on the floor, they realized I was the only woman and would attack me.

I stood quickly and faced the leader. Flashing through my mind what to do with the parcels in my hand—drop them! Felt them hit my leg and clatter to the floor, as I immediately went into a horse stance, solid as I could be, my fists drawn back ready to fight.

No aggression toward me yet, physically.

I punched, and pulled it short. Then kicked and stopped my foot just in front of his groin. I looked him in his light blue eyes, white hair, pale. "I could have hurt you; I chose not to."

He looked at me, then smiled. "I like you," he said.

19 September 91

8:00 a.m. workshop

Drawings into patterns for the next project continue.

Sky

Blue 12m

Light purple 2m

Purple 2m

Magenta 2m

Butterflies

2 or 3

Clouds

Pink 2m

Leaves

10 large = 6m

15 small = 3m

Green 2m

Light Green 1m

Dark Green 1m

Yellow 1m

Sun 1m

Bird

Turquoise 2m

Red 2m

Purple 2m

Magenta 2m

Pink 2m

ISOLATION

Talk with a friend re an Aurovilian with declining health:

long-term care,

lack of caring for each other,

all are pushing it a little in the first place and are quickly drained with an overload.

And then,

1.   I remember the visit of an acquaintance. I barely knew her, but she was very helpful. I cracked while she was there, but because she is not attached to me, we looked objectively at practical solutions to

my problem at the time. And because I was reassured of other possibilities, not a trap, i could get a grip and calm down.

2. After a clinic visit where I had been quite open with the nurse, she passed by one day, briefly. Obviously she was in the middle of many chores that day, but had taken a moment to check on me. I was happy. Someone had noticed i was struggling and just checked. She had not visited me before.

Both visits helped lift me.

2 October 91

Some days—like this one—I feel I need to finish my work here and go.

I'm not sure what it is I have agreed to participate in here, and there is a long way to go yet...I don't want to run away.

Wait. Just wait. A few months more, be quiet and do my work. The joke's on me—it's starting to rain!

The hush of the sea draws near, the soft pulsing embrace of rain.

A breath—a sigh—and then another wave comes by.

A near but muted roll of thunder.

My circle drawing of the sea and stars drifting round me in the wind. Only link the circle now, draw the waves together from both sides.

I am more right alone.

I write more alone.

I draw what I need.

It's fully raining now—and dark.

Among the other candles the big scented one would be elegant except for the dead bugs floating in the molten pool beneath their flame of certain death.

I fish them out.

I want my evening pretty.

I resent bugs today.

The swarm of Kumbeley poochies, the poisonous caterpillars, are burned too. Terrifying to think of their slow wiggly fuzzy grey encroachment on the house. And now I see the roof is going to leak. Maybe. It's damp up there, but maybe it won't drip; it's just dry and needs swelling up.

It's really dark and really raining now, with thunder and lightning. I have everything I need till morning. And then I will be taken for lunch by someone I don't know well, but who seems charming, who thinks of me as a designer (that's all he knows of me), to meet a French designer in Pondicherry and see his work. I will wear something of mine in which people say I am beautiful, and just enjoy the day. It won't be raining then.

4 October 91

God, this is not funny—did you hear that, God? NOT funny. A lightning storm stuck on your house is NOT FAIR!

At the first glimmer of lightning light, I must cover my ears for all I'm worth, or the drums will break. I cried out loud—NO! I scarcely dared stand long enough in front of the windows to shut them.

I, who have loved storms since childhood, am panicking. I worry that the cold sweat on me will draw the electricity in. It's too much power, so close. The lightning cracks in your bones.

Now it's retreating, thunder rolling normally, rain smoothing nerves. Ears are aching with a sharp pain.

My workshop roof is already listing from the heavy rain two nights ago. Will this finish it off? Tune in in the morning.

Hot milk and another vitamin B.

Thursday
10 October 91

Yes, the workshop fell down.

Coping—rebuilding.

Tired, need a day off—how to justify that?

I went outside to do the dishes after breakfast, with bare feet, of course.

A sudden stinging.

A scorpion.

Again.

Off duty. I was sent to lie down with the black stone on my foot. He must have already stung someone else; there's no pain, just a day off.

Thursday
Last in October

Monsoon since a week.

Dear Mom,

I was just in the shower, feeling brave because of the cold and rain of late afternoon, and slightly smug because I was smart enough to leave a hot mug of tea waiting for myself, and my towel inside the house, not outside getting wet with me. And when I left the house, all the lights were ON for the first time in days, since I got your letter, and I was coming back to begin typing an epic letter. The current didn't last.

This will have to wait for electricity; it's too hard.

3 November 91

We are in the monsoon and beginning to go a little mouldy already, probably speeded up by having had no current. This morning I was woken irrevocably by a stupendous explosion, a feeling of, oh shit, lights are gone, xhere am I... Thank you for sending me to secretarial school; I ought to be able to type in the dark, French keyboard or no, and thank goodness this is a manual portable typewriter.

The round sounding of something blozing up

I guess I cqn tqke my glqsses off. It left me lying there going xhat, xhat could have blozn up, then q soft rain; it zqs only thunder; just one. I reached for the lamp beside me; sure enough—nope nothing/ Bqck to sleep/

Yes, I am bqck in Sincerity. NOT at Desiderio's, in MY little house here/ Xe have separated our daily lives, better for us both. Xe xere never really a sompanion for each other, and the habits of breakfqst, etc. zere a good thing for a time, and right, but not nox/ Curious—there is no di,inishment of the real closeness, really.

Lights are back; yes, it appears the different keyboard DOES make a difference. Substitute most of the Q's for A's, X's for W's, also Z's for W's. I won't correct it; it looks more funny like it is.

YOU SAID ALL WHAT THINGS TO MY SISTER last week? These letters take so long, I can't remember; I had better keep a copy.

My workshop fell down, totally and literally. SO, I had to make a new one, which meant first taking the pillars right off the ground, digging new and deeper and better-engineered holes and putting them back up again, getting more causerina poles for the roof (so it can have a steeper pitch) and then woven keet to put on top. GUARANTEED not to leak for three years. The whole process took about two weeks, including delays for rain, etc. All this while I wait for the go-ahead from my client in France, to start the pieces for her house. That cheque, in theory, will pay off the rest of my loan, buy the fabric for the next several projects, and put some in the bank to start my fund for Canada tickets. But because I have to get the fabric all dyed, and they can't do that in the rain, and I wanted to get a head start (so the whole process won't be delayed until January) and the roof fell down, when another woman here in Auroville called me and said, "Please, Susan, can you do these four rooms, at least two by January?" I said, "Yes, OK, but not now because I can only think about one project at a time" (which isn't really always true, but you can't have people expecting you to be a machine and then not be able to do ANYTHING). And "because everyone's mail from France seems to be delayed," she has forwarded me the money. The cloth should be dyed by yesterday, the only trick will be to get it DRY.

There is an epidemic of—oh, what do you call it—when your eyes get totally red and horrible. I haven't had it; John is just over it. Here it is now called MADRAS eye (Madras had so many cases that it ran out of medicine). So there are very many people going around in sunglasses in the drizzling rain, and also staying home with it, because it is so contagious. The villagers believe you can get it from looking at someone. They may be right—and THAT, as much the light sensitivity, is why all the sunglasses.

My vague and hopeful plan for coming to visit seems to be getting more definite. That is, I would like to come this summer (May or June) for a few months. I haven't told John yet that I intend that it should really happen, not be a fantasy. I will do that at dinner on Tuesday. Just reserve a room or two and I will start a plan of action and keep you up to date. I would like to be there for Ashley finishing high school.

It will, frankly, not be easy to do, but I want to try.

I can't manage to say all the things I am thinking or feeling, or planning about making the trip, except that I feel we should come, soon, not wait for "someday."

And how could you know that your letter, with the last lines, "much love—be happy—YOU COULD COME HOME," after having said that you hope I am not settling for the easy way—would come into my hand while I stood in the rain in front of my fallen-down roof, trying to remain amused at the chance for practicing equanimity. I had to get past that one before I could feel, OK you guys, let's get this thing back up and get back to work and generally not let a little thing like this get to us.

Probably I should rewrite this letter in a more orderly, sensible fashion—but I won't.

End of Sunday: house is clean, a little laundry got done (too soggy to risk doing everything), my dinner is cooked and ready for me, the milk is boiled, I have a book, and the electricity seems to be holding. THAT is a satisfying feeling.

Forgive us if letters are sporadic till after the rain (maybe you will end up getting more).

with continuing love, Susan

11 November 91

Dear Mom,

There are letters on the way to you but I have just discovered a nice man at the Guest House who will be passing through to Victoria. He will likely phone you.

I was so excited to get your card and find photographs of your paintings inside. Wow! Thank you.

I am (we are) delighted and impressed, but not surprised. I knew you had it in you. The only question was what style it would come out in. Desiderio wants to know what size they are.

Do you have a gallery in the city already? See you soon.

love, Susan

15 November 91

The storm has passed. We are left with the aftermath of the wake of a cyclone. The lights will be out for days now, for sure. They already were out for days, but then it was tentative.

I've spent much of the day trying to rescue the little ornamental tree behind my house from the branch-cracking clutches of the big tree that I watched fall on it this morning. Futile. It's sad because I only have my little sequiturs to cut away what I can—every saw and cuttee in Auroville is busy with bigger things. And trees are falling before the wind all through the day and more will go, pulled by their own weight from the rain-softened red earth in the night.

All power and telephone lines, of course, are severed in several places.

There are no more candles available. I don't think anyone is hoarding them. There has been a shortage this year, and they are all burned up. I have maybe enough for tomorrow. Tomorrow I will get kerosene for my lantern; that will help.

I swept pathways everywhere through the garden. Everything is such a daunting mess. The old gardeners were heartened to see me after their long long day of sawing, and smiled and picked up brooms too.

The coolness is invigorating. It's easy to eat for a change. I am enjoying that.

The laundry has been out there through all this. Under cover, but out there. No point in worrying about it or bringing it in. It would certainly go mouldy and take the house with it. The sun will come eventually.

Maybe tomorrow.

18 November 91

I am presently addicted to as close an approximation of scalloped potatoes as I can muster—which is pretty damn good. Probably it's got to do with the cool weather and will pass. I am hoping it's fattening. I put carrots in too, if I have them. You should try that. You have the advantage of having an oven, but I'm spurred to inventiveness by virtue of my one gas burner mixed with cravings for variations of potato, onion, carrot ingredients.

25 November 91

The shimmering squiggles gliding across the counter, from this angle a mysterious mirage, turn out to be—with the aid of my NEW GLASSES—simply the shimmying chase of lizards.

Many small strange things will become clear. Will I miss the magic, or see more?

1 December 91

John has calculated the money I need to raise for two plane tickets: an incredible 58,000 Rs in all (US$ = approx. 27 Rs). He says that for that amount one can build a comfortable small house here! But he is happy at the prospect. By next summer it will have been seventeen years since John's been in Canada. Almost as surprising, I have been over here for five years. It's taken me a while to be able to bring him home to you.

The temperature has plunged to a double-blanket, sweater-wearing, rock bottom of twenty Celsius. That sounds kind of amusing probably, a comfortable room temperature, but John remembers that it's only hit that low half a dozen times in all his years here.

3 December 91

Today we go to meet the Director of the Alliance Française about my exhibition.

I am delicately balanced between excitement and an attack of nerves.

16 December 91

Dear Mom,

Thank you! I now have miraculous new EYEGLASSES! A stunning difference in my days.

I had put off writing for a few days, figuring to avoid letters crossing. Or did you get my letter that said I am working on getting John and I to you in the summer?

The voyage plans begin to look more feasible and not just a dream. I am working hard.

Do you have access to BIOCHEMIC TISSUE REMEDIES? Check them out for arthritis (or anything else). They seem to actually work. There is a huge book about them; I enclose "the blurb." Let me know what you think; I will bring them.

Did I tell you? No, I didn't. Separate from everything else going on, I am to have an exhibition next winter (December) at the Alliance Française in Pondicherry. I had been offered full backing, anytime I felt like doing a show, by a business-man acquaintance with enough faith in me to think it not a risk at all. I had to say yes! It's a question of saying YES to life. The show itself will be fun, but it's mostly the gift of being able to work freely, to find what I _can_ express. I am happy. So my year is FULL, starting this minute, starting last week.

Your painting of the ocean view with Wallace Point framing it in makes me quite homesick for the island. You knew that would work.

*****

This is not me dwelling, or worrying, but I was thinking last night, for some reason, about John telling me about your letter to him about the living situations of you and your friends (managing houses, etc.)

We must talk about this when I come (or before). I can see the possibility for me to come back and forth more often over the next few years, and I find UNACCEPTABLE the thought of your being forced to leave the island if you don't want to, because of whatever.

Perhaps what's in the cards is for us to be good and creative roommates. You think about it.

*****

Time to cook.

Give a Happy New Year greeting to everyone you see—from me.

I haven't told Ashley yet that we're aiming to be there. Let me work on it a bit longer. I'm glad to get word of your talking with him, even if he is a typical teenager on the phone.

love, Susan

4 February 92

Dear Mom,

Might as well tell Ashley too now. At this point one of us can make it for SURE. I am working on Phase Two. Second half of the objective.

I am trying to get in gear to dive into the two houses that I am committed to doing work for. The one from France is fully paid for and in the bank. I am trying to do it—her work—without touching that money because it covers one return ticket (just about).

Today I whitewashed the office and have chicken stew ready for John and the kids. The kids are two of Janet's (you remember meeting Janet, where I have my workshop?) and two extra. She's gone away, so I am in her house with four teenagers and two extra workshops!

My hands are full at all moments for the next couple of weeks. The next letter should be a little more concrete.

much love, S

29 December 92

A long gap on paper—but so busy. Mostly all work, with a string of commissions, exhibitions. All attention and energy going toward making drawings, choosing colours, buying cloth, or having it woven.

It's not true there's no play, but it's been on back stages from here to Madras.

Looking out my kitchen window, I see him standing erect with his back to the house. Hood spread, the cobra is protecting my territory. Actually, that's probably not what he's doing, but it's a comforting thought. He's watching the mongoose. Standing his ground, waiting to fight or flee.

2 March 92

Fax to Helen Harper (Mom)

Pender Island, B.C. Canada

Dear Mom,

Your letter was received with much gratitude. A letter follows with the whole plot. I have to make all arrangements and reservations this week. If you can, advancing the cost of one ticket would be a big help: about 30,000 Rs (US $1,000) (to John).

I will arrive at the end of May, in time for Ashley's graduation, if it is possible for me to go. Can you check? I have written to him and said PHONE GRANDMA. John will come about June 10, in time for birthdays. We will stay about three months each.

Next topic: An Aurovilian boy, seventeen years old, will be coming to Canada independently. He is a great kid, very mechanical. We would like very much if he could find work and a place to stay on the island from mid-June to end-August. The aim is for him to be self-sufficient. I think he can fit nicely somewhere. It's kind of important.

Please fax me back on all topics as soon as you can.

We are healthy and good, getting excited about coming. Winter was over in a flash and we won't receive the worst of the heat by coming when we do, and maybe we won't freeze to death there (I will still bring my "winter" clothes).

I condensed this better than I thought; please read between all the lines and expand.

much love to you all,
Susan and John

return: Susan

c/o Centre Guest House

Auroville, TN

14 March 92

Dear Mom,

Wow—the faxes both worked—your letter and cheque arrived, and John and I have reservations (in theory), both for May 30. There. Your money will clear the bank on Monday, lots of time before the prices go up at the beginning of April.

I had written a long long letter to you in and around all the events, changes, confusions, etc. But now everything is just looking fine. I HAD written to Ashley, but the day before your fax, once again I got the letter back, with a rubber stamp that says Moved. Can you please tell him? When you mentioned so casually about talking with him and everyone being excited and happy, I relax and won't worry about him. I just hope for as big a chunk of time as possible.

Now I am nearly finished all the work projects I MUST do, and am trying to organize for when I'm not here. My boys insist they don't need anyone to supervise them. They are right; it's mostly a matter of if I can come up with enough drawings to fill three months. I will let you know when we arrive how all that worked out.

I have just been given Windsor and Newton water-colours, sable brushes, paper, and aquarelle pencils by a departing guest who had bought a lot of my work. Last night I got so fascinated playing with the pencils and brush and water that I burned my dinner (steamed vegetables).

It's Monday morning—piles to do. I like the freshness of the beginning of the week, also. John and I will go to the travel agent after work today and give him money.

Now it seems so natural to be coming. I am excited and happy. Even John said the other night, as we went over a speed bump on the motorbike, "Oh! That felt just like going over a breaker in the rowboat." I won't have any trouble getting him on the airplane at all.

Someone is going to the post office NOW...

love, Susan

4 April 92

Dear Mom,

This is really to you all. Has one of us told you yet that our flight is changed? Now it is 28 May (they don't fly that way every day); stay tuned because we don't have the actual tickets in our hands yet. Yes, they are paid for, and he has made a back-up booking on Malaysian Airlines, so you get us for sure.

I feel so much like writing letters and talking to you all, but mostly have to concentrate on all the work to be done. Janet's workshop (whose "workshop umbrella" I have been under) has, as of 31 March, been turned over to someone else. We are extricating me from the books so that I am on my own. In the end it will be more simple, but right now it feels like an income-tax-type anxiety. The burocracy (see, I can't even spell it) in India is overwhelming—stupid and crazy. She and I got a little nervous this week discovering that she leaves now in under three weeks, her son three weeks after that, and John and I, two weeks after that!

I made John take me to the beach last Sunday evening for just those reasons. But he laughed at me because I got cold in the water. "How am I going to manage Peter Cove?" he asked. We don't think the ocean here is much colder than the air, which, now, after the sun has gone for the day, is thirty-two or so. Better be stocked up on firewood.

Next weekend I have been invited to participate in an exhibition in Pondicherry by a French painter friend. That's OK; it is just one day and will be light and fun. For me, it is sort of an introduction to Pondy for my thing in December. (Yes, of course I'm a little nervous.)

Is there anything in particular anyone wants from Singapore? We should have time and I do have some US dollars.

I won't try to write to anyone else now. We will just be there.

Give my love to the girls.

PS: Janet and I will spend a little time today on WHAT TO WEAR! None of our clothes from here will do. The accountant has arrived; I suppose we have to go fight with him.

see you,

Susan

26 April 92

Fax

Dear Mom,

This one should cause a little stir also.

If anyone feels like meeting Singapore Airlines flight SQ18, 9:35 a.m., Friday, 15 May (yes, fifteen), John and I will be on it. Tickets are in hand.

It's sooner and sooner, isn't it? (That's a direct flight: Singapore/Vancouver, leaving 8:45 on the morning of the fifteenth—less than an hour—not bad.)

love, Susan and John

*****

27 August 92

Dear Mom, the heroic hostess,

Yes, it was strange also to read your letter. I felt like I was still there with you. I knew that John and I coming home to you would be an event, that there would be an influx of relations and friends while we were there, but I hope there was enough quiet time for you and John, and for you.

For me, that was the most memorable, nostalgic, idyllic summer in living memory!

So amazing to think that John had left Canada seventeen years ago, the month that Ashley was born, the month that you and Dad retired and moved to the island full time. And Sukrit, a coincidental seventeen years old, Canadian by birth, but who had lived only in India. So much fun to watch them with "new" inventions they had never seen. The funniest were the remote control and the microwave oven. Much joy, much magic.

I will always remember the moment that Sukrit won your heart by coming into the kitchen and asking, "Do you mind if I make chocolate mousse?"

It was such a grace that both the boys seemed to be so at ease with each other, AND that they pulled off getting the summer job across the bay at the resort.

I wish I'd been there to witness Ashley's swim around the end of the island and across the harbour. He's clearly not my baby anymore. I know he's still partly a boy, but I am happy to see the young man evolving.

I really was glad after we left that the boys would still be there with you. I knew that the house would feel different but probably nice—a different phase, a different grouping—starting with only John and I, and easing out of the summer at the end. Good.

We survived the flight. What else can you say about that trip? Except that the Singapore connection was extremely smooth. Those people seem to have thoroughly grasped the fact that tired travellers are not always capable of rational thought and organization. Right off the plane they point you to the NIGHT STOP desk and your worries are over. You would love it.

We didn't sleep much in the night, but felt relaxed and intensely grateful to lie down. Especially our John with his shingles.

He started treatment for the rash as soon as we got back. It's really going away. Less and less painful and he's not so tired. By the time this reaches you, he should be OK.

I found it very shocking landing here. It was very hot, muggy cloud covering, trees dying from the drought, so many people down with fever, no electricity, and home alone.

It was difficult, but the hard part passed after about a week and now my various enthusiasms are coming back. I think I must have left them over there when we got on the plane. "They" say that all parts of our being don't travel together; "the soul comes on horseback."

It was much easier to land this time knowing that I can go out again when I need to, or when I'm needed.

It rained a good hour and a half two nights ago, and is trying again now. Wonderful cool breeze, but everyone is so sleepy from the unexpected low air pressure.

The workshop is underway again, at full tilt. I am so relieved that I <u>feel</u> like doing it. My tailors made it through the summer, but the work needs me. We learned a lot about what to do next time I go away.

Tomorrow I will start the large drawings for my next commission. It's so much fun to do several hangings in one house, to make an atmosphere that enhances the living space. I try to get my own wishes out of the way and catch the feeling of the person I'm doing it for. That in itself is rewarding for me. A joyful experience.

I will give you more workshop details after I am really settled, but it looks like we are "on a roll"!

I have started work on the *Drawing on the Right Side of the Brain* book. I find it quite exciting.

Time to eat, I forgot (in my determination to be a prompt letter answerer). It's not too late, just well past dark.

with much love, Susan

September 92

"Derek Bollen and Susan Tait had a very successful showing at Stonecrop Gallery on Pender. Susan's double voile hangings and Derek's definitely different landscapes of Pender sold well."

(p. 10, *Island Tides*, August 27, 1992)

4 October 92

Dear Mom,

The stamps on your last letter—Emily Carr—are so beautiful. I gave one of them away as a special gift.

Thank you is a little word for the letter, photographs, and cheque, but thank you.

Your report of the scene (or non-scene) at the airport when John and I left you in Vancouver would also fit at the end of a novel by the *Accidental Tourist* author. Are you able to find it at all amusing yet? Next time we really should make a video.

John wants to know if you rescued the chamomile he left behind in a brown paper bag somewhere or other? On top of the fridge?

Did you have a little post-holiday holiday yet? Are you painting? I think I told you that I have started *Drawing on the Right Side of the Brain*. It's already helping, especially when I am making the big drawings from small size. When

I start to feel it's too hard, now I can say to myself, "No, Susan, no drawing is any harder than any other."

YES. I will do the exhibition!

Monsoon is trying to start. Wonderful things are blooming and growing like mad.

My first design in STEEL has actually been made for the big arched door to a friend's house (the drawings I didn't get to while on Pender.) I can't help it, I am excited; it's beautiful. I will take photos.

The picture in the newspaper from our small show while on Pender looks not bad, hmm?

Don't miss me too much, I'll be back.

with love, Susan

19 November 92

Dear Mom,

Yes—thank you—your letter arrived before my birthday. The "thank you" should be written much bigger.

I am getting down to the wire about the exhibition—you know the stage, when the real Work begins.

Back at the workshop after a full day in Pondy measuring windows for new client, photographing his house for backup of my memory of the rooms, visit with him to grasp the feeling of his wishes for the hangings that will enhance his home. Not so exhausting when there is a quiet place to rest in the middle of the day. Then Friday morning: work-shop, afternoon library, evening make dinner with a friend. I look forward to Sunday and I can STAY PUT.

The weather is like heaven; we are between storms. The cyclone missed us last week, but was still a big mess. The sea was magnificent. Roaring so you could hear it easily from up here on the plateau. Another storm is due, but this week I will do my laundry anyhow.

Did you ever read Steinbeck's *East of Eden*? I imagine you must have, but I have just discovered and devoured it. So rare, books like that. If you haven't read it, do—or do again.

Yes, tell me about your happy feet!

The very loose sketch on the front of this letter is not a Christmas bulb, but a crystal prism, about the size of my loosely closed hand, that Desiderio found for my birthday. It is fascinating, very old. It is capped with silver and has a chain to hang it from. Perhaps it had been hung in a temple somewhere so that it could be touched in passing, because it seems worn, as with age. It is very very heavy, and a beau-tiful treasure.

*****

John reported last night that he had written to you and mailed it. He mentioned, in giving you "the news," casu-ally throwing in the last line about typhoid. I nearly decked him on the spot. Difficult, though, where to draw the line of "news-giving." Yes, five people with typhoid in a population our size is epidemic proportions. Yes, the wife of a close friend did die, and it was deeply shocking. But the typhoid didn't kill her by itself; she had not been well for a long time. The others are recovering nicely.

We are well, taking care, not eating in strange places, etc. No new cases.

*****

I am trying to finish this and get it in the mail.

Sukrit, who is trying to write to you, came to tell me today that he is going away for a few months, to a place called Coimbatore. He has a chance to work for, and learn from, a famous race-car builder/driver. He had told me some time ago, but then it was almost a dream fantasy for him: the ultimate possibility. He goes in a week. I will take him to dinner on Saturday with John.

I am enlarging the last of the designs for the window and door grills for a friend's house. Whew! There are twelve different sizes and shapes, therefore twelve drawings to do. The designs have similar properties to the ones that I do for fabric, or that someone would do for stained glass, except that the flat bars will be bent to the shapes. Each room in the house will have its own flower theme, from lotus, iris, ending with bedrooms upstairs; the master suite has sweet peas (the significance of which is Gentleness). We are all very happy with them. I couldn't have imagined how very graceful my designs would look in wrought iron. And they are absolutely one of a kind, for the drawings become the pattern, which is burned away in the process.

We know that a lot of Auroville mail isn't getting through again. Steps are being taken to try to remedy it. Clearly yours are getting here. Thank goodness.

I haven't heard from Ashley, but dreamed him so strongly around my birthday it was like I could just turn my head a little and he would be there. It contented me greatly to be told of your phone call with him.

Exhibition crunching close. But the rain seems to have stopped, so the lights are on. Bad that the rain stopped, but good for the lights.

Time to make dinner or it will be too late—again—7:07.

always with love, Susan

PS: Registered so I will think more positively about this "getting through." xox

21 January 93

Dear Mom,

Whoops! A little time warp just slipped by.

Yes, our postal system is working. I think, though, that the registered letter took a little bit longer. Now you are well into your Mexican holiday; are you being flooded out? That's what we hear from here. Although I know you hear from there, dreadful reports of what's happening here. We are absolutely fine.

I am recovering from something, however. Yesterday I hurtled to Madras and back. I'm sure you still have the memory of that airport trip engraved close to the surface of your brain.

So, tomorrow I will continue; now I will drink my hot milk and get into bed.

Next day, afternoon, at the clunker of a typewriter on library duty.

Category: Home. Work will apparently "just begin" pretty soon on the part that will be the kitchen and bathroom and sleeping room upstairs. Afterwards another L will go on the other back corner with sitting and study rooms down and sleeping "up" for me. That part may take a little while, but when the first part is done there can be a REFRIGERATOR. I did (you know me) manage to get a little worried because I don't have money to contribute now—but it seems it's all going to happen anyway. There are lots of other ways I can contribute, and lots of work I can do during the whole show!

I laid the last of my worry to rest the other day during my laundry-washing time in the garden when I realized a funny thing. If I were a married woman, under official, traditional care of some man, I would not even question living arrangement changes that included me!

Oh! Another time warp. 30 January 93

Workshop: suddenly I have a new "office," designed and built in the last few weeks with the "Lego method" of bricks and keet and a lot of openings in the walls. This, also, was not instigated by me, but by Janet's expanding plans. It's a good thing, really, because it gives me a real voice in my corner of her "territory." I may choose to move my workshop later, but for now it is a very good challenge for me to remain calm and just carry on with my work.

Since I started this letter, the foundation for one half of the house extension is DUG!

Card from Satomi from the Caribbean on her way back to Vancouver. It seems the fantasy trip we spoke of last summer is actually on her agenda. I will tell you when I know more than that.

I aim for getting to you in the summer of '94. How's that?

On Sunday I called Ashley. I got through on my first try, which meant I woke up his dad at 5:15 a.m. He was pretty good about it. Ashley sounded great—lots of music, studying—just going to get up anyway to go skiing. He did ask about the cost of tickets to here, which means it's on his list of things to do. I really don't mind if it takes a little time. It's just quieting for me to know that when he can, he will come. I guess you understand that. As long as it doesn't take too long, right?

Some people—dancers—are coming in a few minutes to discuss costumes and stage sets for a performance at the end of February.

The first thing we have to invent is a thirteen-metre-long WAVE.

I give up! I surrender my whole workshop to these games for the rest of the month. I'm so happy that I've held to my decision to keep myself working as a studio rather than a factory, so that I CAN be free to play, to be fully creative.

What to do? It's going to be Auroville's twenty-fifth birthday on the twenty-eighth.

I'm also going to give up trying to tell you everything in one letter. There is MORE. Whew!

love always, Susan

PS: How was your holiday? Hello to the neighbourhood!

3 March 93

Dear Mom,

Time only for a note. Desiderio's mother has been here since the beginning of February. One more week out of my house with a girlfriend (girls' camp). I have barely had a moment to notice or have it matter where I crash my head down at night. We have just spent several weeks madly doing the costumes for a wonderful dance performance, put together with the raw material of Aurovilians, by a thoroughly professional American dancer who lives and works with the Carolyn Carlson dance company in Paris.

We all worked day and night—it was an enthusiastic success. Now we all have been asked if we are willing to take it to Bombay and Delhi later this year. The director has also asked me to work with him on another BIG project. I will tell you as it unfolds.

I don't know how this next bit can possibly be Part Two; life is getting like a fairy tale.

Remember that I'd told you about the possibility of an adventure with Satomi (who I'd worked with in Vancouver, ages ago)? I got an emergency fax from her last Sunday (Auroville's twenty-fifth birthday) asking me to phone her collect immediately. She must go in April to deliver the GENUINE ALASKAN PUPPY (that she went to Alaska to get) to her brother in JAPAN; she has invited me to join her there around 19 April for three weeks or so, so that she can show me Japan!

I have called her and accepted. Can you imagine it?!

I will keep you posted.

> With my love always, Susan

17 May 93

(*on notepaper from Kurashiki Kukusai Hotel, Kurashiki, Japan*)

Dear Mom,

Back from Japan, straight into the thirty-eight-degree soup.

That was a tremendous experience, mostly beyond words. Yes, the cherries were blooming, and azaleas wild in the forests and everywhere—I mean everywhere. Hydrangeas as I never imagined they could be, and freesias making me think of Vancouver. But the peonies: I was stopped in my tracks whenever I saw one. Sort of an awed and in-love feeling. They made me want to paint!

*****

Small break to bandage a mason. Hydrogen peroxide is always fairly dramatic—magic almost. I've told them that if they get wounded and don't come straight away, then it will be "bubbles" medicine!

*****

In the telling of it, there was a lot of food (I don't think my appetite has <u>ever</u> been so good). Many beautiful shrines and temples, wonderful speedy quiet cars and trains (most speedy).

But the thing of it, really, was to be completely out of any known routine, to have all control of the situation, and responsibility, taken from my hands, and yet be safe, cared for, and catered to. I couldn't even talk to anyone except the hostess and a friend of her brother, who watched over me the last few days in Tokyo. I could only surrender.

Now back to work. Except that it doesn't feel like back to anything. Rather a new start. Even my workshop is in a different place. It's in a compound with a friend who has a group of weavers. I think you would love the huge wooden looms that are big enough to do the largest bedcovers. My new studio is simply beautiful. Simple is the key word. A smooth cement floor and brick wall just the right height for sitting on that goes most of the way around. There are the typical granite pillars and a tall keet roof. And this time, I have the luxury of an actual storage room big enough to have my steel cupboards to keep all my precious cloth away from moisture, mice, and other creatures. It's a little further into the greenbelt, just a short bicycle ride away. It feels like a perfect fit for me. And at home, the masons are out there putting the ceiling/floor between the new extra downstairs and sleeping room upstairs on the addition. I just went out and gave them all hats.

23 May 93

Longer break. I have written all my thank-yous to Japan. Many. All of which, of course, will have to be translated by someone. What an amazing gift, out of the blue, an invitation like that—to JAPAN. Stuff of dreams.

I have spoken to Ashley. He will be staying in Vancouver while doing his audition for a jazz studies degree. So I guess by now you know all the news about him. Music fest in Edmonton.

A very strange thing has happened. The police have recovered my stolen camera, food processor, flashlight, and umbrella. Tomorrow I have to go to court and sign them out. That, knowing India a bit (as you do), is a much simplified version. And I hadn't even realized that my umbrella was gone. What do you expect when it hasn't rained since last November?

Much love, and aren't I always promising a more together letter soon? Remember, I just had to write six coherent ones for translation!

PS: Did you get over the "What am I doing here?" feeling after being ill when you got home after being here with us? I think it's normal. Here, we refer to it as LANDING.

love still, Susan

13 June 93

Dear Mom,

I have reverted to ballpoint pen because it's the season of severe smearing (of ink). We've had a couple of hour-long, deliriously welcomed downpours. Just with that much, the gardens look so happy.

We are getting to our summertime skinniness, but eat like mad every time it cools a degree or two. Tuesday, John and I had dinner with Sukrit. Lemon pie by Sukrit was an event!

Have you ever tried:

1.   Cider vinegar and honey in hot water? Delicious and it helped me.

2.   A friend swears that bee stings help. You just have to catch one and put it in a glass upside down on your hand.

3.   Applying softened comfrey roots is said to lessen pain.

4.   Take apple cider vinegar baths or ginger root baths. Drink a small amount of ginger tea while IN the bath. Drink burdock root (or burdock burr) tea. One cup, three times a day, for a month and a half. Alternate with other cleansing teas and use detoxification procedures.

Numbers three and four are from my herbal medicine book, which I like a lot. The burdock strikes a strong chord because of something I found in Japan.

I'm sure you have advice coming out your ears, but you have to get that arthritis OUT.

John and I have just received our birthday present. Be assured that it will be used for treats and funny nice things. Thank you.

It has dawned on us that it ALREADY is a whole year since we were there. So quick. That means I will be there again with you just as quickly.

They (the masons) are preparing now to put the roof on the addition to my house. Now that I have my camera back from the police, I will take photos. Be well.

Love, Susan

31 July 93

Dear Mom,

Happy Birthday!

This is the balance of my mystery bank account on Granville St. in Vancouver. I'll bet you never ever thought you would be receiving money <u>from</u> India!

Maybe you can have a little lunch or something on me.

with my love
forever
Susan

TWO PHOTOGRAPHS

Looking at these two photographs I feel a mystery. I don't know if it's to be solved—or just watched.

What is motivating the identical deep concentration? Quiet, centred, somehow subconsciously pulling together to be in place to survive with unexpected joy—catastrophe.

The bonding began with a small dream. The boy took her hand to show the way on a path. And another night some months later, another sleeping vignette. He came to sit by her on a bench in the tropical forest.

Time passed. A more disturbingly real vision. A dance.

SECOND TRIP BACK (PRESUMING THAT HOME IS AUROVILLE)

1994

Madras, Bombay, Amsterdam, London, Vancouver

Another circle, with exhibitions along the way to pay for my ticket. A superb way to travel.

It's two years since I came back to the west coast. Finally allowing myself. Any sooner and it would have been a running away. Now I feel settled enough to know that I can go and come back.

Ashley will graduate from high school. Filled with pride for him, I take another small plane to his more northerly home. It's strange to be invited to stay with my son's father and his new wife. Oddly relaxed, our attentions all turned toward the boy we've shared. He took the stage with friends, at ease with each other and the full auditorium, and played the saxophone that already he had held for years. At home with it. Then he lounged on a high stool, alone, and seduced us all with brilliant vocal jazz. I feel my life complete with his completeness.

The next day Ashley and I somehow are home alone. Friday.

A phone call from my mother. John is trying to reach me from India. ODD.

I can't imagine what he could want that he couldn't just tell Mom.

Sick—injured? Something's happened. Perhaps he's only missing me, or forgot to add some suddenly vital thing to my list.

Dialling the long string of numbers, I cling to thoughts of bungee cords, a really good spirit level, or the special sun cream.

The pulsing international echo, bouncing the words, again, again. Siva's killed his wife. Desiderio is sending you a FAX.

Free-fall to a vacuum of somewhere I've never been. An immediate madness of words I can't take in. And still there's more in his voice, something he can't say.

Are you all right? I need to know. Yes, I'm all right. The fax will come. He will explain. I feel John helplessly holding me over the long-distance line.

I crumbled to the floor, a brainstorm drowning me. Ashley gathers me up and in. Mom, mom. I finally hear him. Mom, everything you've ever told me—do it—do it ten times—now! Calling me back. Weak tears now, confusion at the body-blow I'm feeling.

Stunned, a robot, I wait till Monday. They help me wait. Awkward, lost, pour me a drink. They don't know what else to do.

Moment by moment the weekend passes. Elastic cords tightening around the globe—tightening—attached to my heartstrings, drawing me home—the far one.

I'm pacing. Unreasoning grief.

I'm haunted with a jolt of remembering the dreams of Siva. The incomprehensible—why? The power of these feelings of loss.

I wait. Numb.

The fax is stuck behind locked doors until Monday.

What else has happened? Someone more is wounded—I know it. I try not to think.

*****

The Fax

Breathe.

Your Siva has killed his wife. The children are all right. He is in jail. Your workshop is padlocked and your workers sent away. He is in jail.

I have just fallen off the roof of my house and will be in bed for a few days.

Dadu, whom your brother was taking care of, has died. The villagers are on the rampage in the greenbelt.

But don't worry; it's July.

Breathe in everything beautiful you can.

With love,
Desiderio

I fly

Back.

A HARD LANDING (BLACK HARDCOVER NOTEBOOK)

Thursday morning
11 August

Write it?

Yes, I am angry and hurt. No, I am not being centred and graceful. You shut me out when I need letting in, in a safe place. I will stay out of your way with his mess I'm in—everybody's way. You're right, there is no previous experience for what is happening now, no ground rules.

I can't find a way to be. You can't help.

I never wanted to be a weight on you. Believe that.

I feel like crashing my head.

I need to cry and have someone hold me for a while. I am tired of rituals of calmness to sleep. Rituals of sane things to start the day. The most cheerful normal things I can think of—hoping for a smile in the morning. I know even as I come like that, I shouldn't—because I'm not quiet and you can't stand it, don't want it, aren't interested.

You are injured too, immersed in physical pain.

Oh, why bother to try to explain. I can't anyway.

I feel like going away. I feel like screaming. I want to shut off my mind, stop my heart. It's emptied. I don't see the point of continuing. Where to go?

I don't want to be alone any more.

How can I feel guilty for not being able to manage?

11 August 94

Dearest Ashley,

What a messy way to leave. Even my phone calls didn't go through. I so much wanted to talk with you again. I guess you weren't home from your concert. I called you right up to my plane.

You'll never know how much it meant to have you there with me when I was falling, how proud I am of you.

I will write when I can, as this unfolds.

unending love, Mom

12 August 94

Today some calmness—be quiet in it.

*****

John is here.

15 August 94

Still here—we are waiting.

22 August 94

My dearest friend,

So much upheaval has happened that I can't remember what, if anything, I've told you. Desiderio is back at work after his accident, but moving slowly and with pain. The most important thing is that he CAN move around now,

My workshop is still "on hold." I don't know what I will do now, but am trying to be quiet (get quiet) and stay open to what will come. It has been a very painful difficult time since I got the news in Canada that, as well as Desiderio falling from his roof, Siva's wife is dead and they had put him in jail. Just in the last few days he is out and I know he is on his way to see me. They were holding him far away and he has been having to sign in daily with the police. He can come any moment. There have been so many conflicting stories, I must just wait—not easy.

And then, for the past ten days, my brother has been staying here with me. Now he's OK, but he was delivered to me in a kidney stone crisis. There were a horrible few days and nights. Now the worst is passed and we have done all the tests and are looking at choices of treatment.

Somewhere in there I had Desiderio cut my hair. I was feeling too grief-stricken and worn out and a little frightened and looked all those things. Now it's not too short, but much more curly and happy-looking. I will give you all my hairpins and jewels when you come.

I will tell you as things unfold. Right now I can't even speculate. The thought of you is a comfort to me.

With much love,
Susan

Monday, near the moon of September
5 September 94

Last night I woke to the dog pack growling, light in my eyes. I don't know how the moon got so big so fast. It's not good to sleep with full moonlight being the only thing covering you.

I moved into the shade and the dogs abated.

Once I had a dog, a big one, who would stand over me when I slept and growl softly deep in her chest when I was dreaming. Last night wasn't soft.

Siva has come straight to me as soon as he could. Such a mix of feelings. I am so happy, so relieved to simply see his face. But we're crying; we're sick and scared. Our eyes are shining with tears that never stop. I feel I will never smile again.

I listen to his story. The argument they had—the not speaking, her cooking dinner in a temper, and the sudden fire. The panic, running for a car to get her to the hospital—her death.

The gruesome story.

Siva's gone again, but will come back, and I try to sleep. In the night I wake, sitting up in bed. Shaken. Trying to think clearly. I realize the dilemma I'm in. My intuition is to believe what he told me. I also realize that I WANT to believe him. But what if he lied? Then, in one way, it's simple. I throw him out. That also would mean that I can't trust my own feelings—then what? But what if he didn't lie? Then what?

I know that I have to gather all my courage and detective powers and check the small details that are always present in a story, that CAN be checked.

It takes some time, and help from one friend who has the fortitude to not desert me. We do check, and he did not lie.

So now the battle begins.

It's September; I've been back for a few weeks only. And an exhibition has long been scheduled for October in Madras. I don't have a workshop; I don't have any tailors. The only upside of coming back from Canada so quickly is that I carried work back with me. A start.

Siva and I confer. He will work; he will get the others. I don't know if we can continue, if the workshop is finished forever. But I have a feeling about this show coming up at the Alliance Française in Madras. Just get me there, I tell them. Something will happen; we will get a sign, some direction. We start. I have little money for cloth, less to pay them. Never mind. They are clinging to me for their lives, we work to save our sanity.

We begin still sadly. But determined. One more breath, one more day. I have no ideas, no feeling to create, but the work is saving us. We are mad in a way, I suppose. I can see us, sitting cross-legged in my room. I search the trunk of hangings so carefully put away and we begin to cut. We shear the cloth apart, and put it back together into floating kaftans. We make more and more—it's magic.

One day, a small smile.

The date draws nearer. Normally Siva and the boys would come with me, to help, and for fun. But this time, it's out of the question.

I must go alone.

Madras Exhibition Designs

Harmony

Peacock

Elephant Ear Leaves

Goldfish

Small Psychological Perfection (plumeria)

Psychological Perfection

Psychological Perfection (blue)

Protection (bougainvillea)

Moonscape

Surrender (rose crystal)

Radha's Consciousness

Beauty in Art (peony)

Island Rain Mountainside

Sun Moon Earth

Totem

14 September

When I left this morning for Madras, the jasmine flowers garlanding the rear view mirror were dewy fresh. I was also. They have passed beyond limp to crisp. I have gone beyond crisp to limp. The driver has managed admirably—only a slow wilt.

Tuesday

Desiderio saw the unspilled mirage of tears flood my eyes—and knew not to ask. To find some other distracting brightness to burn it off.

I carry the exhibition with me, pressed and folded, packed in every corner of the taxi. It's a long road.

Dangerous, frightening, but an insulated, isolated, calming bubble in the car all the same. Nothing to do but be.

The Alliance Française: an imposing, white, French colonial, run-down, elegant building. A mansion. Front doors opened to greet me. Posters and banners announce my presence for the next week. The house is yours, I'm told, as the staff all leaves for the weekend.

I'm not quite alone; a friend has come to join me, and help with the setup, the organizing, and the butterflies of stage fright. Ann is, by chance, a psychologist. French. That's good. Both those things are good. But I'm without my boys—the ones who know me so well at these kinds of times—who know what to do, how to hang things, how to manage me as we get close to opening day. The normal case of nerves is there, as usual, but the weight of Siva left behind, and the whole story, is so heavy. I am trying so hard not to let anyone see. To appear normal. Professional.

The exhibition is beautiful. We fill all the rooms, making a world of gauzy colour moving in the breeze, staining the air with shafts of colour. It changes as the day moves into evening, spotlights making a soft, wild, atmosphere. We have the place to ourselves. Completely. Someone has made the decision not to advertise for the opening, because they want it all to their own diplomatic selves. We wait. We go out for lunches and spend time with a dance troupe putting on their own show inside ours. We spend time with a martial arts master, practising our Kalaripayattu moves. Ann is a marvel of psychological uplift. The days pass.

The last day, just a half-hour before the end of it all, Yamuna appears. She appears astonished by the whole display, and also astonished that no one is there. A Madrasi woman of action, suddenly not a stranger—she is firm that I must approach the director immediately, arrange to stay another week, and that she will bring me the people. I do. She does.

Before we know it, a newspaper reporter appears, and a television crew. Yamuna, about to become a close friend, insists again that I must come back and do another exhibition—in six weeks, at her home.

The sign is clear.

We will continue.

11 October 94

Still. It's the day after my exhibition should have closed—but here I am.

While here, I've been asked many questions, sometimes involving a deep look.

How to proceed? Moment by moment. Wait without waiting.

My companion, my help, is called back to Auroville, the long drive down the coast. I will be left alone.

Missing Siva, drawn to his heart by the sadness still clouding everything, I want to call him to me. She laughs as I tell her that I need him but won't call because I feel it too deeply. The stupidest thing I ever heard, the psychologist in her says.

Almost immediately I am called to the office of the director, to the telephone. Siva's voice is on the other end of the line—the first time I've ever heard him on a telephone—telling me that he is missing my face, is too alone. "Get on the bus, come. Help me take this show down and bring it home."

There. Another step taken.

I am being pulled more deeply into India. Now I'm surrounded by powerful women of Madras. Led to us by some alignment of the stars. Businesswomen who, it seems, recognize something in me, perhaps as simple as another woman fighting to survive, determined to right wrongs in my personal world.

Siva arrives hours later, and crosses paths with Ann; we all lunch together and do a changing of the guard.

Once again, I wonder how many times I will experience the delight of his presence. Unexplainable echoes of dreams float to the surface of my mind. How much trouble am I in?

The afternoon passes, with the Alliance staff less practiced than we are at taking down and stowing an exhibition. Hours of careful ladder-climbing, unhanging, folding, putting away. Gathering props, curtain rods, ropes, paper-work. We know what we're doing, and are good at this.

I meet again with my new Madrasi cohort to cement our plans to come back. It's fresh and exciting, this opening world. I'm still frightened, fighting the sadness, trying not to panic—but in her eyes there is a possibility that there is a future.

On new footing, Siva and I dare to go for a small celebra-tion dinner. The daring is in the fact of celebrating; we've had dinner many times before. Now we've had a sign, a strong signal to fight, with our weapon: the creation of beautiful things. That is what will save us.

The night approaches. The Alliance is a cavernous build-ing; the staff all disappeared till morning. My quarters are huge. I've travelled with many shows before; I would never have sent one person away because they were an employee, or a different colour. We would stay together; it's a road show. A dilemma. I'm not in Canada any more. Another barrier to take down, a taboo to undo.

In the natural way of grief-struck and far-away-from-home human beings, Siva and I become lovers. Naturally.

Morning, as I wake from a deep, relaxed sleep, brings a moment of panic. A really big "Oh, no, what have I done?" moment. But it's done. Our reality has shifted. I wait for the lightning to strike and it doesn't. There is a beautiful dark caramel-skinned young man holding me easily in his slumber. The dreams have found their way past the surface of night to a solid waking fact.

And now, the approach to return to our community— where Siva, and I by association, are in an exile of sorts. Painful. Take a breath. Many breaths.

It's a long road down the coast to home. We hurl ourselves down the sodden highway, puddles deep and potholes unpredictable. Driving monsoon. We have hours during the journey to plan, to gather strength, to be together until separated by the circumstances of our living.

There is a new show to plan for, to do the work for. There is publicity: television, magazine and newspaper articles praising my work—and opposite that, the isolation.

21 October 94

The *Hindu* (India's National Newspaper)

Friday Review: "Beautiful Creations"

"Ravishing," "enchanting," "fabulous"—these were a few of the uninhibited comments of some of the viewers looking at the creations of Susan of Auroville at the Alliance Française Gallery, which were on view recently. These were not tapestries in the conventional sense because no weaving was involved. These were a somewhat novel idea in textile hangings, which can be hung in front of windows, doorways or even as room dividers. Susan used to live on the West Coast of Canada before coming to live in Auroville eight years ago. She enjoyed working with textiles even when young and she has been trained well in stitching and tailoring also. Her mother is an artist and that made Susan familiar with colours too.

Susan's creations were composed of pieces of different coloured textiles cut to specific shapes and stitched together to form patterns. When in Canada she used to work with thick materials. But when she came across the light cotton voiles in the varied vibrant colours of tropical India she was simply fascinated with them and started using them in her work. Once, as she watched the wind sway a textile hanging, in a flash it occurred to her to use two layers of screens back to back. Susan first makes a small drawing in which the overall design is divided into several segments and each of them is allotted a specific colour. This drawing is then enlarged according to scale in the actual size in which it is to be used ultimately: on this, small pieces of the coloured materials are pined on their respective segments.

Originally she was doing the stitching, now she has assistants who do it and they cut the materials exactly to the required shapes, which are stitched together. The work is quite exacting, since the shapes have to be cut with clean edges, the curves neat. Since there are two layers, two pieces of each have to be cut in such a way that when they are arranged back to back they would fit on each other exactly. The stitching has to be neat with the same width throughout. Susan uses different colours of material for the same shapes on the two sides so that when viewed from one side the other colour is seen through: according to the available light, and particularly when the breeze blows, the hanging creates very attractive effects. Susan wants the light to penetrate through the material, but she also wants it to move in the wind and that is why she chose this medium rather than stained glass, she declared.

Each piece takes considerable time to make. Susan uses very interesting colour combinations: for instance, in the Peacock she had used different shades of turquoise blue with reds and oranges in the wings and on the reverse there were different shades also of the same blue but not those on the front. Some of the pieces she prefers to be viewed from only one side. In some she had made a dramatic combination of rich purples and beige and in another shades of earthy brown along with golden yellow. She had attempted landscapes with hills too, with a rising moon. The two layers were attached at one end and hung on a pole so that the patterns on the two sides coincided.

Some of these screens come in pairs so that they can be hung on two windows or doors. She had created even a sky canopy. The same idea of attaching different pieces of cloth to form a pattern had been done with raw silk too, made up into wall hangings, cushions, and dresses like kaftans, vests, etc.

As she tries out the colours in the sample drawing first with watercolours. Susan is slowly getting into painting too, but she wants to resist the temptation as she wants to carry on with her present work. -L.V.

9, 10 & 11 December 94

Invitation for next Madras show: Chetpet, Madras

Susan Tait from Auroville

presents

Transparency in Colour and Line Design

Using cloth in a stained-glass effect:

Voiles & silks exquisitely transformed into an extravaganza of see-through hangings, room dividers, window blinds, lighted panels and also exclusive clothes for women who dare to wear tent kurtas, swirling skirts, ornamental vests, kaleidoscopic kaftans, etc., etc., etc.

2 January 95

It's not over yet. I seem to be on an accelerated pro-gramme of almost too many stock-still, back-to-the-wall, rapid-assessment situations. Do I stand here and scream, do I rush forward with a big stick, die on the spot, or do I laugh with the magic of it all?

1 July 95

The peacocks come—an iridescent stalking through shafts of morning light. I like it when they come to me after everyone has left for the day and I am here alone in the garden.

6 December 95

According to the Runes, this is the time of the prince and princess coming together to live happily ever after.

I am not a young woman by western standards, but I am in the east and there is magic.

There is a quiet urgent call at the door. Come into the garden. Cobras. I drop my work and follow the gardener, our bare feet quiet along the brick path. In a shadowy clearing we stop stock-still and stare. The snakes are there. Together. Two of them, twined and writhing, raising their bodies a metre straight into the air. The sensual strength of them is breathtaking. Their hoods are spread. It's a dance.

We are very close to them and they don't see us. Or they don't care. The gathering semicircle of watchers is transfixed. I can feel us each trying to appear casual in the morning warmth. That this spectacle isn't affecting us deeply. An animal moment going on and on. This territorial ritual is rarely witnessed. We should leave.

JUDGEMENT DAY 96

The last court day before the judgement.

Morning—I was fine.

I will cook something good and nourishing and warm for dinner. It's not trite at all. Nourishment will be needed—for me too.

Maybe this is the place to start telling. Before it was too hard for anyone close to me to listen. Too scary—too close— too far. A nightmare, but forbidden dream moments that I longed for.

Now it's only for the magistrate to free or convict.

I had dreamed of Siva, years ago, beside me, in our work, walking with me, taking my hand to show me the way, dancing a grand waltz—and making love. Siva.

All along I knew they weren't just dreams, because of the way they touched my days. It had begun.

Where I came from is about exactly as far as possible from where I'm sitting now. It was just off the southwest coast of Canada; I am now just on the southeast coast of India.

But waiting for Siva to come home?

Two weeks ago there was a fight in his village, resulting in the death of a political leader.

He'd not been there at all, but suddenly, as happens in villages, there are several categories of men who can't go home: the ones who were involved, the ones who weren't but who people would like to get involved, and friends and relations.

Desiderio suggested that Siva stay here. Many of us have someone tucked away. Not sure that he meant for this long, but I'm relieved to have him close during this time. Safe.

He was attacked on the road last week, while coming with his cousin from the court. His motorcycle was run off the road at Irumbai, a quiet stretch between the palms and casuarina forest.

I am choosing to believe it had nothing to do with him personally. The air was wild.

Yesterday, November nineteenth, the public prosecutor was sacked! Not just from this trial, but completely. Siva's had to go again today. It should mean the thing is just over except for formalities. He's been gone all day, though.

Even here, with the courts and police so corrupt, when there shouldn't even be a trial, to be accused of murder is not a joke. And I can't do anything.

He's told me his dreams—waking from the touch of his wife, coming to sit by him in the night. Checking to see that he's all right. Asking her, "Why did she do that?"

We've talked openly over the last two and a half years, and stood by, stood firm.

29 November 96

Judgement day. It's 5:35 p.m. and he is not home yet. I'm trying to stop waiting for the car.

It didn't come. No one came. Raju and Jyothi's cycles stayed outside my house overnight. I'd sent both my other tailors as support for Siva. I couldn't be seen to have anything to do with it.

I did all the meditation—lamps lit, incense, Rescue Remedy, hot milk, wrote to friends who are "skilled listeners"—no sleep, or sleep between nightmares. Some violence has happened.

30 November 96

Raju and Jyothi come at 9:00 a.m. to bring me Siva's jewellery and shoes. He's in jail.

The clearest I can make out is that the magistrate has said that Siva did not do it but he is giving one month punishment as an example. This is incomprehensible.

Steadfast women friends are giving pure comfort. We're through the worst of it; now it's only waiting. I am assured it will be fully cleared by the end of the month even though it's ALL WRONG. MAD and STUPID.

I did eat, for Siva's sake and Raju and Jyothi. Me, I don't care.

I did sleep, feeling him beside me. It's cold now. I am mostly worried about how cold he will be. I will make him a hot bath the moment he steps back in my door.

1 December 96

7:10 a.m. Raju and Siva's younger brother, Rajavelu, is at my door. There's a note from Siva: Please, I will go to the lawyer. Tindivanam, one hour by bus. Yes, of course. When he left to track down and speak with relatives I started my day again.

I told Desiderio what I knew—not for discussion, just for information.

Take care of myself: hot bath, oil, dressed. Strong quiet feeling of determination. When the going gets tough...

I held that all the way to Tindivanam with Rajavelu. He was doing it too. He's a straight, clean, good young man. The second brother. The next in line to carry all this weight.

The Minister's house: the veranda, police guards, dozens of supplicants and another dozen inside the open door. Seated behind his desk in an armchair with a brocaded purple wool shawl. Cool types by the doorways murmuring into a cellular phone. Passing it. Sunday morning politics. We waited. Not long. The lawyer came out and told us quietly that the Minister wanted to go somewhere. Heart sunk. "Come now." Heart rose again.

In the back room, we asked, what is this—how can this be—innocent and in jail?!

NO! The judge has imposed the extreme penalty: life. Life in prison.

NO!

I can't hear him say that. I can't understand.

I am wooden. I am dead. I can't manage. I don't know how. I don't remember how to breathe. I see Rajavelu's face. It is the same. And I know we have to choose. NOW, die right now, all of us, a flash of collapse, YES, or survive—somehow—and GET HIM OUT.

The Minister—I don't know how we got there. "Don't worry," he says, "don't worry, don't worry, don't cry. We know he is innocent. There is no evidence. We are appealing. The magistrate, the idiot, the cipher, he doesn't know the law; he will be GONE in three or four weeks. Don't worry. Don't tell."

Don't tell. Siva doesn't know. He's the one in jail and he doesn't know. The lawyers are launching the appeal.

One moment at a time—one breath—don't start screaming. Breathe.

I need some help here. I could talk but I'm not allowed. I need the comfort you give to a young child who can't speak yet. You just hold them till they sleep. And you don't let go.

John is here.

Spilled all the beans.

But the official public version is the crazy one about being innocent but punished just in case as an example. And let the lawyers do their work now.

Eat something.

2 December 96

Krishnamurthy, Siva's first cousin, came and I gave him a woollen shawl and a note. Only told him that the lawyer said, "Don't worry." I send love, and the lamps are lit.

Raju and Jyothi came, but late. Raju has a fever. He looks like he has cried. Thank God for the language problem. I tell them the lawyer said "Don't worry." They are visibly relieved. Now me. This time round I know a little of what to expect. When things are very difficult, a lot of people don't know what to say and, therefore, "can't see you." That's just fine. I will be able to use that.

Afternoon.

I made it through. I went out and made it back. I had to face Aruna last night, and another friend today. Both were with me on the first day of full confusion and panic, and knew I had, without a word, taken off yesterday. No one knew where. They let me tell them, looking straight in their eyes with a plea not to be pushed further, that the lawyer had said "Don't worry."

Now Jayaram, another cousin of Siva, and a dear friend of mine too, will come. Because he IS worried. And I will try again. If he cares enough about us both, he will accept that also.

I don't know what to do now, today, this afternoon. What I want is a month, at least, in the hospital under heavy sedation.

3 December 96

Still waves of the urge to collapse. But I am trying to work. I am managing to get convinced that we are caught in the middle of some political madness. Fighting won't help, only knowing it will pass. The quieter the quicker.

I count the money in my bag. Passport and eyeglasses will have to wait. My papers are not in order. I can't run home.

There is work. We have cloth.

5 December 96

It's been in the newspaper. Of course it has.

Lost at sea. The waves are further apart, but deep and strong. I think I look all right. I can talk, mostly. I want to sleep.

Keep the work going. Jyothi will get my food. I'd better learn Tamil pretty quick. I see Jyothi and me willing ourselves to understand each other. Raju went at noon to Siva. What a gift to be with such men so closely.

Susan

Scleranthus

Cherry Plum

Wild Oat

Chicory

Vervain

Rock Water

Water Violet

My friend made me do Bach flower remedies and sat over me.

7 December 96

It's raining rain and leaves and thunder sounds. Cyclone playing off the coast.

Monday, a quick e-mail to Ashley. I tell him we're in a leaky zoo here at the moment.

Jyothi and Raju took Siva's gold to sell on Saturday. Sunday report from Jyothi when he brought my chicken, sugar, onions, and matches. Pondicherry is closed. Jayalathitha, Chief Minister of Tamil Nadu, is in jail.

There is a meeting at 3:30. Five Aurovilians have been given Quit India notices. Next Saturday they must go—unless we can do something. It seems the whole world is mad.

Rajavelu says the lawyer has gone to Madras, on his own initiative, about this matter (our matter, that is). The family of Siva's wife is ready to help.

Tomorrow I will go to see Siva in prison.

One friend has offered to come and stay with me—another has said that I can come and stay with her.

I have to take our Jayaram to Madras to get his leg adjusted. Somehow in the midst of all this I've been appointed caretaker through his ongoing struggle for the correct artificial leg. Through my work, and exhibitions, I've been sort of adopted by a very wealthy dancer, who just happens to own an artificial limb hospital in Madras. She is fascinated by Aurovilians, especially the artistic foreign ones, and wants to learn about us through my eyes. I will use her contact also.

I've been paid enough from a commission of silk cushion covers to renew my passport.

It's still raining.

12 December 96

We are all fine. Not personally flooded out. No fevers.

I was thinking we should try to phone you on Christmas. You will know when you get this; I suspect that open phone lines will be like needles in haystacks, but I will try.

E-mailed as often as I could to Ashley through the RAIN.

December still

I've barely made it to the health centre, slumped gingerly on the back of John's motorbike. I'm waiting for my viral colitis to be taken care of, in the lineup with those with typhoid, cholera, on and on. A man walks in with a small woman, supporting her carefully; he has a plastic bag with a dead snake in it.

Straight to the head of the line.

31 December 96

I didn't understand fully before about keeping a lamp lit for someone.

25 May 1997

Monday—noon

I've been home for three years. Three years since I had a workshop to go to, since I was supposed to be anywhere. I suppose it looks like I've turned into an eccentric creature. And now it's half a year already that I have been home alone. I can go freely—I am free to wander—but I'm not bored of the lines of my surroundings. I am not a recluse; I'm a bit reclusive, perhaps, but people do come (only the ones who are not afraid—or don't know).

BLUE "PAPYRUS" NOTEBOOK (GREEN COIL BINDING)

10 April 97

Pondy

Shoulder bags loaded

heavy

with practiced balance

slalom the lorries,

plodding bullock carts

silent lightning

Say nothing

Watch and hope

Race it home

With relieved sighs

Slip the weights from

Our backs—from our minds.

MORNING EXERCISE NOTEBOOK

10 April 97

Don't just lie here, write it down. Financial service—can they take my cheque? Business and judgement—go to the bank with it. Too tired—taxi. The bills the bills the bills...sit down, figure it out. No money for Siva today: tight. It will be all right—or not. Work.

Call to Mani the mechanic—cool and odd but he is cool and odd. Nothing in that for me. Mysore, go to Mysore. The taxi a dark fast box hurtling down the road. My art teacher houseguest is coming today and there is no food. I don't want noise. The kettle will boil now. Why does this exercise stay in my head? It can't go rolling forever in the head if it's coming out my fingers. Remember that—lie down and sleep a bit after this. Tea is steeping; it will be all right. The new lawyer is confidence-making. The bad lawyer we're trying to get rid of is hysterical—little man, what is he frightened of?—more than me, I think. Visa coming. The ninth was a "good day to take action." I didn't feel like it but perhaps underneath it was right.

Maybe it was good to see the definite flippedness of that man. Siva's brother wants to go away—eyes bright past the airport, like a small boy watching the planes go. Too long to wait for Siva. Keep waiting. Keep being here. What will happen? Who can tell—God can tell. I need to go through this part. Jayaram's leg trip today—whooshing back and forth past each other on the road. My head is still on the road too much: too much money, too much time on this— work—next week again. The art teacher today, and bank, food. Dentist, not today. Blue glasses with beautiful light, shining like an ice glow. Your eyes showing delight. The look of young or ancient delight in the turn of your hand, moving it to the light, lining it up with your eye. The smile, as if you found it yourself—glad.

Monday
7 April 97

Monday morning is daunting, too big; the paper is too big, the day too big, the sky too big. Birds are in the air, sea is in the air, sea is in my ears, the birds are not stopping. Sleep is not stopping; I want it not to stop. The lawyer on the phone, lawyers in my head—too big, too much for me— one phone call at a time. Madras madras madras mad mad car ride, tired. What to do? I don't know what to do. When in doubt, do nothing; is that why I'm doing nothing—too much doubt? Fill the page, fill the day, empty the night—the night the night. The book—write it, paint it. Dogs barking, still the birds. Somebody hold me; take the hurting away. Be happy, remember laughing, remember the joy of working, joy of drawing, happy tiredness, big satisfied feelings...only work, only the work—is this how writers do it? Write, just write write write write write write write write write write write write.

Footsteps outside—the sea is roaring, crickets are boring, electrical sounds in my ears, dreaming, trying to come. My head, it is too busy. I wake up talking. Page two is coming; these pages are too big. Take the boat, get off at the Island. Writer's cramp—relax, relax, relax. The village is waking up, dogs are barking, I have to go to the bathroom; I'm allowed to stop for that, I think. Move that hand, move the pen, empty the head. It doesn't matter what side of the brain you're on; don't be angry at small wrong things, be angry at big ones that don't hurt myself any more. Use the strength, use the weakness, don't stop...you can lie down but don't give up now. God will do it if I keep awake, keep turned to the light, keep open, keep praying, light the lamp, find the happiness in the air. Don't worry, don't think, don't plan small plans; plan big ones, do it—do the adventure. Unblock unblock unblock. Nothing to lose. Floating floating floating floating floating.

One more thing to do—OK, I've been doing nothing at all. Scared stiff means stiff stiff—a big shock means paralyzed, scared to move, scared to stand still, scared to be me—too hard, too big. Maybe it will be over soon (the hard part); I never will be over the great adventure. Ha! Tired—just an excuse—I don't know what to do. Paint in the hours—there are many hours. Get the paints back. Nobody get in. Write lightly, pressure hurts the hand, the head, the heart—let the pressure go. Have tea, laugh at the bright things, laugh at the devils. Fight them hard, fight them soft—fight them. My friend who died did. Your bright room's at the end. We walk to the light only at the end. The tunnel is always there, the bright tunnel of the path; stay on it, don't get confused, only fight to stay on it. My only job is to be me—a whole perfect strong powerful creative and loving me. Other friends are lost, too much hurt too far away. Leave it leave it leave it— floating floating floating—slowly, not in panic, not worry, not hurt; be free to fly (no strings to tie me up), fly my life, my life my adventure—my God—run through me.

Tuesday
8 April 97

The bones of my fingers are slipping down, condensing. A shorter and shorter virus—nothing to worry about. Lawyer thoughts—I wake always with lawyer thoughts talking, tired to my bones. I don't know how to get relaxed or happy—I'm so tired—maybe I will die after this work is done (it would be much much much easier). I don't want to be here anymore. Another big friend finished; she is too closed up. I thought she was my big friend—she was, she still has that feeling when I pass her on the road, with her overenthusiastic big smile. I would smack her again. I listened for years to her, her mood out over this and that, but she had a wall that I couldn't go through. It must be also my fault—am I blind? Am I too radical? Siva—I feel nothing now. When I see him, yes; when I get a letter, yes. Light the lamp. Too much tiredness in the air. It doesn't matter if I feel nothing (burned out); I will see this work through and get him out of there, then I can let go of everything. Will I fall down, will I break, will I crack or dry up? The most frightening is to dry up. To condense, to blow away, a dead body on a bier of flowers on the road.

I wished through the tears, sobbing tears, that it was me. I'm losing heart. Scared scared scared scared scared. I wake up, head buzzing with talk, too serious for too long too long too long. I don't feel well. Try to let it go. I try to relax, don't try very hard to work; I don't know how. Little moments of happy. I don't know what to say. Try to pull out. Talk to the neighbourhood shrink—tell him. Tell him I'm scared, tell him my heart hurts, tell him I'm too tired and that I don't know what to do. Look for a break in the clouds; catch the sunshine. Hold the light—hold the light, hold the light, hold the light, Mother, please help please help; I will try to be open enough to receive it, to know you are helping. It must be difficult for you to do anything through the gloom. Please help to lift it. I will try to be quiet. Flowers, sunshine, health, food, rest, work a little, just go through. Help is there. I will clean my room—shelves are a mess. A day off from worry—no shouting, inside or out. I am getting hard to handle. Light—soft—hold it, stand in it. Let go let go let go let go of hurting feelings, light the lamp, put out the incense, write the letters, eat the papaya. I release this situation and everything connected with this situation and I ask for guidance, guidance, guidance, guidance. I want tea; I'm thirsty.

It's not hot this morning—why not, why is it cold in the night? From the rain? Who is chopping wood out there? Roosters far away. Birds filling up the rest of the air, bees swarming in the night. I'm almost done, almost through, almost finished. I don't like the rooster sound; it's a common noise, a harsh life reminder, and the dogs and the far-away truck sounds too. Hot and hard out there. Also the sea, in the other ear background, roaring all the time when the day is quiet enough. Keep it quiet enough. Where is Rajavelu? Do I have to pull him every single time? Do I have to chase him down? I'm tired of that. That is finished.

11 April 97

It's not necessary to do this the very moment of opening my eyes; it's all right to be a bit comfortable first. Tea, some cushions, a non-torturous route. The art teacher is a soft presence in the house. Everything will be all right. John is wounded on the foot; I didn't even look—is he all right? He is all right. Now today what? I can rest, better rest; don't panic. Why did Jyothi not come yesterday? Why is his baby sick when they are trying to get those papers for Siva that say his baby is sick—karma, or what? Siva will be angry. Are things changing there? Of course—what will happen? I don't know; is he getting removed from me? Before when I woke in the night my mind was saying "Siva"; now my mind is saying "lawyer."

I have a list of things to do. I am angry with all the energy flying about, all the lying flying about—and all the flying about. I shall fly in other directions. I can't just sit waiting for everything to be the same; it won't be. I have to be on my feet and walking to meet my destiny. My destiny is not just to wait. But waiting and holding firm is part of it—to be removed and hold firm at the same time. Move in an upward direction, and not just to tears; the warrior, the gentle warrior must be there—she is there, she will not be consumed. Put an ice pack on that leg; it's not better. I'm too stubborn, giving too much away that I don't have. Have some fun, hop on the train, go to the coast of Mysore—Kerala—accept the invitations. Go to Mysore when the teacher leaves. Jayaram has his new leg (feet out of stock), but he can use the old one. What to do next? Something nice, something fun.

12 April 97

Why in Pondicherry is there nothing to do? No reason to go—it's too hot. There's no lights. It will be hotter. My life story can't come out in a room full of women I don't trust. A couple of them I trust—others I just like. But that's not the place for the WHOLE THING (deeper tone of voice). No, I am not afraid or closed at all, just—why? I myself don't even need to remember all of that; it simply was part of the murkiness to come out of. Sky-gazing, peacock blasting the morning, moving by candlelight. I can't see this pencil writing—which is just as well, because we're not to look for a long time. My head is full of dense air, pressing in from outside also. Siva, what is going to happen to us? I miss you, but now I am a little angry. Maybe this distance is right, to readjust the world. No Pondy—the rest of the week is too full.

Sunday Monday Tuesday Pondy, Wednesday Madras— again again again. Peacock crying—really crying. Today is heavy-feeling. Why Pondy? To eat a big lunch that I can't digest, in the sun? Get more fruit. Jet lag from the ferry. The shops are dark, with no fans—hot fans and A/C but not completely. A lot of dreaming. Probably because of so much talking these days—so much Siva situation talk that I can hardly recover between the days. My leg is burning inside. Be still—be still more than I even want to—stay home stay home stay home. Do the home things today, don't try to run around or the big collapse will come. Harbouring strength means staying in the harbour, mending the nets, painting the boat. Feed the warriors, let them sleep and search for fresh troops—don't put out to sea or you will be beaten. Mend that boat—fresh tar on the hull.

Afternoon

I am more concerned with not being able to find the darn thing on my kitchen floor, after it had landed on my neck (it fell off the ceiling, I suppose). I brushed at something; the scorpion blended with the tiles.

Over to Desiderio—please, can you help me find it? I can't see well enough.

Don't you want me to take care of that sting on your hand? I hadn't noticed.

Sunday
13 April 97

Shadows over my writing when I sit this way make it an invisible thing, the shadow of my own hand. Six o'clock, not five like last few weeks. The feeling of dread before I go to bed has lifted. Sleep is clearing but the bed is too hard, like everything else has been. The bright thought of our art school, not the hysteria in the air. It sounds like pure fun. The walls of water, walls of cloth move it all around, change it, push it, bend it, melt it. I can't get stuck with a feeling like that. I think she really meant it about the students and faculty, finishing the thing, making it work—free. It's a freer impulse than fitting into some stiff stale thing already complete. I always wanted to go to art school, to be part of that bright world. Now is that being given to me, not just as a place to go, but also as my place—a joyful rightful play place? I don't have to be a grown-up—not a stuck, fixed, rigid adult. Better not. All the things I'm not good at are not my way. Maybe then I will also get fuller, bigger. What to do? When Siva's free he can come with me to that world; it's his place too. I will write to him about it—something to dream about, a good clean future thing. We can exchange somewhere else in the world also, some sunny bright place, with stone carving, statues, painting, writing, sculptures soft and hard, large, now in the air, an opening in the clouds; light will come down all over the place, washing it all away—tingeing, at first, the dark corners with a little bright-ness, then moving and growing into a luminous world. We can be shiny. My work can be to shine—to polish not with a surface shine but by melting the murkiness away. Turning shadow places to light, letting things be as they should be, dispelling the gloom bit by little bit. Let them melt together; let them torch.

Monday
14 April 97

Tamil New Year, therefore a holiday. Why exactly is it now—why so many new years? My head was rolling with worry thoughts just now when I woke; I forget that it's all right, everything. Money is OK. Write to Mom. It's two days to her operation; tomorrow she will be in the hospital. Is my leg attached to her? I don't think so but something is wrong in there. Warm heavy air, full of birdsong. A small breeze is lifting. But it's so still; it feels as though electricity shouldn't even be getting through. What do I mean? Are we allowed to wake up first and get comfortable? Yes—this isn't to be a torture-only first thing. Pain is in my leg; today, manage that—exercise or not to exercise? Not to exercise. Actually, I like the little watercolour sketches. They're barely there, but they feel hopeful. I will be able to do that too—I can I can I can I can I can I can. Painting—yes, I can paint. Ha! No, I won't boot out our teacher. I like her.

The dogs are barking. Different birds have woken up now. I want to get my hands on the green cloth from Madras; I want to wear it. It is pretty. I want to look pretty and free. I want to be lively, I want to move freely. I want to let go of the pain in my body. A different kind of letter to Siva—he must not panic, he should not blame me if this thing is taking long. I do all I can as properly as I can. We have to hold on, have faith, pray, understand even a glimpse of what is being given to us now. Paint, draw, write—not madly, joyfully—hold the joy that IS there. Follow that line. Melt away the tight parts: pray pray pray and relax.

15 April 97

Oh, good morning. I'm mixed up about the days. Rain is threatening, but it's all talk, I think. Peacocks are abounding in the trees. Great distress with all this mating business. I need more corn for them. I'm starting to really want popcorn but they are getting it all. I made a little painting start yesterday by myself. It feels good to do that—I can do it—it will come from my hand. Siva—pray, be quiet, lawyer tomorrow. Organize that work; organize my part of that work and then let it go, with no worry. Organize what can be organized and let the rest go. Take time for me, then no one will collapse.

Warm and slightly cool nearly a breeze (not wind). The rising sun over the ocean; I can't see it yet but it's getting lighter, pushing the last of the night-cool air, pretty soon that is finished for the day. Birds too are relishing it. The reading lamp is warm on my shoulder. Tomorrow Mom is operated on; now she is in the hospital. We are ahead with time, so she is there. Will my leg get better? I will phone the other leg hospital with Jayaram and make him talk (he must do it)—he is getting heavier and heavier and heavier. I am getting lighter. Siva's brother—find him today. Do I have to chase him every time? Not every time; he will come.

Lawyer phone calls: just do it, by rote, but pray behind and around and over it. Just do it, and make a list of other things to do. Thread, sample colours, quilt batting, silk, thread for canopy, lampshade basket, photos, iron clothes for Madras, put buttons on, find lunch, do my nails, relax about it all, buy aspirins, be happy. Write to Siva—he's not lost, is he? Do I have to be ready to fight? I will fight for life, fight to let the joy be, be a gentle warrior, be a warrior, be unstoppable, get shining, keep shining, keep moving. No frustration, no blank walls. Make some tea, smile through the day. Tears should be finished. Amen amen amen amen amen.

16 April 97

Madras morning. Five o'clock leaving—now waiting— what is happening to that boy in there? Getting a little long...does he need rescuing? Is that my job? Will the man explode if I go in there? I think so. I'll leave it till I finish these pages. The lawyer is saving his ego, I think—or talking his way out of the mess he has made. A warm and sticky mess. Opportunity to be a hero. Let's go somewhere for a cold drink, somewhere with a toilet. Relax. Glasses are sliding down my nose, vegetable sellers cycling up and down, calling out one vegetable at a time. Onions have gone by, and tomatoes—and something in a sack, I couldn't tell what. The music of Bombay through one of the windows. Siva at the movies. A strange man just went in that door— not a strange man, one I don't know. Here comes one more vegetable. He's going slowly, maybe it's eggs—but I know that word in Tamil and it wasn't that. Don't think, just write. He's at the door, watching me. I guess he's just waiting too. Time is going by.

There are no loud noises from there—no noises at all. Does it matter how long it takes as long as it does take? Better write a love letter to Siva—tell him about all the good stuff waiting. It doesn't matter how long it takes; we are living. A breeze is moving but that's all. What to say? Nothing, just do this part, do the list. Go home and paint, draw, cook the dinner, sleep, work. Find the joy that is waiting to land on me, on all of us, that somehow surrounds this whole situation. Patience is the reward of patience. The reward of patience. It is an hour and twenty minutes—is he all right in there? And am I all right out here? I think yes, pretty soon I will check though. At the end of this lawyer chapter or another scene. Calmer now (me, that is). Do you think I can use his bathroom?

17 Friday—not Friday—Thursday

Sort it out, get it simple, write it down and leave it—write it down and close the book and move on with the day. Long calm letters to Siva, separate the topics, get it clear, write it, send it, don't worry about the consequences. It's his karma too. Just keep mine clean, keep it clear. If he comes out for a day or two something bad will happen, like sex for the thrill, for the drama, is different from the deep loving that arrives when making love closely—different from chasing desire. That leaves me empty. I feel him panicking. I know the mood. I know the feeling. Drop it drop it drop it—make him understand that the work for him, for all of us, for justice and freedom, is there—we are doing that for love. If you push us through panic, it won't work when you get out. Our work is simple; be quiet, not down, not low, but strongly quiet, if you can. Know that this is wrong, but look deeply to find what ELSE is going on—how you can use this time? How it can make us stronger? How we can be ready for the new world when you are back? If you waste the time being angry with the world, with those of us trying to help you, then the time when you are out will also get a lot of energy wasted on clearing feelings from this time. We all have work—the hardest—to keep on with our daily work also. The practical main reason that work has to be done properly is to have the money to work for you. If your brother, for instance, doesn't carry his work well, he will lose his place and not have the money to do what he needs to do—for you also. The strain on him is large. He is handling it well, but if you shout at him he will feel hurt and sad and it will be very difficult to continue. I have told him it's normal for you to be pushing, of course, and not to be hurt if you shout—we are the only ones you have to do that to, to try to understand more from your side—and to keep on doing his good work and not be afraid.

18 Friday

Look at that: I skipped right over Mom's operation—how can I do that? Madras, I was in Madras, in the car, picturing her being pain-free, relaxed in the hospital. Immediately she should be better. Today I will write those things to her. She wants letters more than phone calls; they are better in so many ways—you can keep them. Touching matter—we are losing it, the more e-mail, servants, convenient things of life. More important to hold, to encourage, to grow. The artists—the old ones who still touch matter—remember, and keep that thread urgent urgent urgent. The painting will help. Make the pocket for John myself—will the machine run? Get it serviced—cleaned, oiled, running—do it myself. Bring the other one back from Yamuna. Can we take another tailor? Should I, can I, can those two keep on holding on? Wait, don't jump yet—don't get confused, just keep going. Don't expand on that side—expand to round out the rest of me first. I can also do the work myself. Finish the quilting, touch it—hands on, brain off. Move it, carry it, touch it, put me in it. Start with the pile of cloth waiting; make the skirt, make the pareo—remember my hands. Find that way again—go slowly, find the way—do it step by step. I can.

It's not lost, only rusty a bit. Unlock all the doors. The cloth—touch it, work with it—it will work with me. Free a different way by writing, free another part with paint. Take down all the walls, all the barriers. Leave no barrier to the light that wants to pass through. Be a free channel—practice. Clearly. Let the resistance go. There is time—there is time only for that, only for that. Be a free channel for light, for creativity to flow through—listen to what the universe wants to say through me. Exercise all my parts—all. Be a free and open, clear and beautiful channel for the light of the universe to pass through my eyes and hands and heart.

Saturday

I see that red cabbage in the kitchen still—it is going beyond decoration. I don't want to eat it—too dense and dark, too dark red. Why did Siva's cousin come yesterday? Murky, not clear—who died? Why were the police there? Is Siva coming tomorrow? How will he come? Will he be quiet? Will he go back, or will he go forth? Can he be simply happy to be free for a day and then go back? Is he lost from this world? What will happen if I touch him—will I break? Will I break down or break off—break away, break up or hold together? What is happening to my workshop? It can hold together. Are the stories they have made too confused—are they mixing up the karma? Should I show my little paintings to Desiderio? Something is in them; I want to look at them. I want to make the habit of putting the brush on paper. Can I catch enough of that while our teacher is here? Open that possibility, bring it down to a material beginning. Learn the basics so that I am not afraid, don't hold my breath. Maybe I did this before and forgot about it. Maybe now this

Susan Tait Charman

is something I can do very well. Begin, grounded. Slowly, so I don't panic or get overwhelmed. Get the learning so I don't worry when I put the paint on the paper. I know it's there, waiting for me to pick it up. Just do it, open my eyes and look, pay attention, learn, don't be scared; there is all the time in the world. You know what scares me? When you say it looks like I have been doing this for a long time; it is a weight on me to do it well. I don't want to be awkward or clumsy; I want to do it easily, I mean flowingly, but I need the grace period of being a raw beginner. But when I look at the others I can see from the start a greater ease is there for me. I don't want to be mediocre at this kind of thing.

20 April 97

Siva is free.

Siva was here; he is gone and coming back, and going back. Somehow inside himself he is free—free as me. Awake with him in the night, asleep with him in the night. He doesn't disturb me in sleep; it's a comfortable thing. This leg is hurting but has a good reason. I will just be quiet. A lot of people are around—too many, at moments, but those moments are also all right because those good people have come. Sound from next door—Desiderio starting Sunday— sound from the village and potash, sound from the fridge after two days quiet. Sound from the birds, sound from my stomach. No morning tea next door today; keep these vibrations here—over here—it's quiet but excited. Castles in the air, castles on the ground—bring them down. Matter — silk and satin, beautiful lustrous things—welcoming, cheering, laughing, cheering up our celebration of the funny life. Siva is gone to reassure his escorts that he didn't run away. He's making his rounds freely all day(his word for it is "rounding")—get those English books for him, got to study, got to write, got to work—ready to work. Jyothi, Raju, do it with me. A tent for the school. Next winter school. My bird of paradise, Siva, keep shining in the light; your mind is like that. Like an angel in the trees flying, so quick and graceful you can hardly follow, but quiet at the same time. You were completely wrong to suggest we part. We are raising up beside each other. Clearly there's a lot you didn't understand—the subtleties and the freedom—you only saw a small corner of us, of him and me. I withdraw from you. I will keep the contacts but at more distance. I will tell who needs to know about this challenge. It is not a dark secret; I will fly with it. We are alive. More alive than ever. There are no problems, only creative solutions, it's true. Let the magic roll, from here on in.

Monday
21 April 97

His sister died (on paper only) so he could be free, for three days. Jiggly inside today (liver)—we didn't eat dinner—stupid—or better that we would have eaten nothing instead of all those fried things and a glass of gin. Today fruit and salad only. Keep quiet, work on the castle, do the pyramid sorting, do nothing at all, drink tea, lie down, wash the floor. Talk to neighbours. A shirt for John—a shirt for all—how can I feel hungover from eating fried snacks? Cold chills. I do not need to have a fever.

Paint today—one flower, only one flower, just loosely, don't tell anyone—just do it. Do everything. Writing this morning, scribbling away straight out of sleep, unscrambling all the night thoughts. Put them down—don't look, don't read it, write to Mom. My ears are ringing, but it doesn't stop at the ears. Aruna is so beautiful when she smiles; she smiles all over her body. Dear Siva, sweet boy, hungry—he is lovely, soft, shining—I could see a new strength growing in his face. Nine or ten months only left on his loan payments—finished, free from that one—both free, finished. A burden lifted through persistence. It can be done; we did it—finished, free—his face had a glimpse of the determination I saw in a black and white photo I'd taken. No one is bothering him there. He told me he has been warned, no one will touch him at all, because that look can come on his face; no one will touch him. No one will ruin him. We will go away somewhere, together, after this chapter is finished.

22 Tuesday (the next day)

Cold—do I have one? It feels like, seems like...I don't have time. Eat neem leaf balls, gargle, tea, tea, etc. Blast it out—too much going on here—congestion. Attack in the news—is it on me? Feels like. Push it out, push it out; it's not to do with me. Even if it is, it's not true. I release that situation and everything to do with that situation and I ask for guidance. I release that situation and everything to do with that situation and I ask for guidance. I release that situation and everything to do with that situation and I ask for guidance. Mother, please take it away. I will do my work and leave that part. The castle walls—think of the hangings for the castle walls, the pyramid—maybe the tailor didn't cut one colour? Maybe that's where the missing colours are. Sort it out now, do it now and get them started. Bring home the pattern for the skirt and do it myself, fill up the gas bottle. I can go with the art teacher in the car. Check the money in the bank, check the money in the Boutique, check the curtains with Raju—why aren't they done? Find a way to keep quiet in the day. Do the castle walls, make the drawings, find the sumptuous cloth (satin, shining, khadi, solid)—make them grand. Make them joyful—make it gasp-ingly beautiful. Make it rampant enthusiasm. Make it.

23 April 97

Start the fingers moving, stop composing. Wake up—
headache, a little—cold is there. I am cold, chilly; it must
be me—because it is not. Clear things today; my head will
clear at the same time. The music was too loud last night.
He doesn't know, must have needed it. I will make a sound
barrier; it's louder at night than Sundays. Saturday will
come and take the canopy away. I can't imagine what happened and anyway, what rain—we had no rain here. Plan
the Hyderabad castle drawings today. Clear my head,
breathe easily, clear my head. I don't know what to say.
Stopped—blocked. A cold will give you that feeling. I release
this situation and everything connected with this situation
and I ask for guidance. Letting go, help now. Letting go,
help needed. Drink of tea—get jaggery—better than sugar.
Do it, drink that. oooooooooooooooooooooooooooooooooooo
ooooooooooooooooooooo

ooooooooooooooooooooooooooooooooooooooooooooooooooooo
ooooooooo Slow, those circles. Does it have to be words
I put down? I want to lie down, to stop. I won't, though;
is that the whole problem? Where is Rajavelu? Did he go
to Villipuram courthouse? Does someone always have
to push and pull? Can't everyone just do what is needed?
New cushion covers—they need it. Spruce up the cushions,
tighten—they're spreading all over the floor, I feel. Fatten
the cushions—get 'em stuffed, get 'em soft—softer, anyway.
My bed, too. Now it's better. My leg is better, all is better.

Hard knot or ball in or near my heart, though. I don't know what it's hiding, I don't know what it covers. Dissolve it.

Thursday
April something, 24?

Cold miserableness—how is this possible? Sniffy, stuffy, croaky, a little headachy, achy—but I seem to look nice in the mirror, pink with a small fever. Be still—go slow, don't spread this around. Siva in jail. Jyothi today. Client, send money, should send money. Check the Boutique, draw the castle, dream the castle. Send it off, send it off, release the dream into the air, let it be free in the universe. My thumb joint hurts, fingers are stiff. Why, why, why? Relax, just work. Why is there so much noise and talking outside this morning? Is something going on I don't know about—don't need to know about? Get Desiderio to look at the peacock, send a note to John about dinner. I want my morning hug, but won't take the germs over there. Close the teacher's curtain; she is sleeping so nicely, and anyone can come now. Oh, what to do today? A letter to Mom, a letter to Siva, drawing for the castle—no rush, no fuss today. Have tea, drink juice, get fruit, eat (not much); let this cold go out. Oh, sniff, oh moan and groan a little, oh just go back to sleep. That's not it. Finish up small things—clear out, clean, organize what should be kept, throw out the rest. Just do it, from top of the pile on down to the bottom.

Friday
25 April 97

Oh, good morning. This doesn't seem very profound, or high or spiritual, but that will come. Will it? Will it? There it is, that simple. One thing is clear to me; I cannot eat like that. Everyone should just relax and realize that thin is OK. I am healthy, and if they stuff me my body doesn't want to do it that way. Kidneys aching—lemon water today, a good cure. How did someone get bitten by a viper? Did she see it? She was scared with all the medicine that didn't work. How can people get so stuck—well, that's a dramatization, they're not so stuck—on trying to fatten each other up? It's only out of care; I am happy to feel so loved and cared for. Siva has lost weight (he needed to), now he is good. Just keep him healthy, get him free. Can I continue to pay? Yes, nine more months loan at least—we can do that, pay it off. When is the first Sunday of the month? Check the calendar—don't worry about it. Spend some time with my client in Madras. This time, don't rush back. Be free, find the paint store. Sort the photos, use the new album. Go out, drop in at the library, check the Boutique, come home and work. Stay home, be quiet, draw for the castle—do the elongated lion dragon drawing. Dragon, lotus, crown of India, dragon lion, winged lion—is that done, is it correct? Check the drawings—stretch it out in graceful long curves, border, get glue, put the paper together. Ask Raju for the glue. Get some more. Stop eating eggs and chocolate. Stop eating fried things. Drink the lemons, eat banana and papaya, juice today, tofu OK (but fried stuff not OK, it doesn't go). Write Mom, tell her just don't worry. I am a little thin, but never mind. I don't want to carry any more. I am perfect, strong, powerful, whole, creative, loving, and happy.

Sunday
27 April 97

Sunday is overridden this week by the airport trip to take the art teacher back. There was no early Sunday morning time; we were in the car. My mind is trying to worry again. Money, bills, fridge empty, what to do? Shift the priorities. Siva has to wait his turn. We have to do this in a different order. First Raju and Jyothi; they are working, they must be paid.

ooooooooooooooooooooooooooooooooooooooooooooooooo ooooooo My head is rolling full. Release the situations, all the situations, ask for guidance, and get to work. Get food, take a rest. My stomach is upset—vomiting feels like it will happen (too much heavy input of food). The rest is OK; we are all diving into this big adventure together, everybody getting calm, everyone getting together. Do we need outside threatening reasons to do that? It seems so—but maybe we can get in the habit of doing the parts together that should be done together, no time for games with each other. Some separation should take place—no fooling with that either.

But the supports must not fall down. We need the bridges, to bridge the gaps. There are bridges and catwalks on the cliffs, no need to panic and just jump off into the deep void. Calm down—all those big stories are nothing in the end, only how I handle them is important. I am not superwoman (but then again, maybe I am), but maybe I can grow into one if I let it happen, if I cooperate, if I let the energy flow through. If I don't stop it, block it.

Oh, I want to lie down and close my eyes again, write to Siva, check the plans for the garden pyramid for Madras project, write to her, tell her I am well, finding my feet in a new way. Changing stages. This diving-in holding-on stage has shifted. Grab hold of my own life; I can't just attach all my energy to her as, perhaps, was necessary in the beginning. I'm glad there has been for all of us this time to step back from being overwhelmed, caught in the drama. Now I must pay attention to my work, my other work. Bring my machine back. I'm ready to work here. I need the backup here. Not gathering dust.

Tuesday
29 April

Morning head exercise. Late this morning, but late according to whom? Slept long—exhaustion. House is tidied a bit, inside and out. Jyothi and Raju off to work. I will get down to work, but first the clearing of the head. Today I will do it methodically, slowly, no running in circles or even straight lines, no running; move when ready, not before but also not after. Nothing for nobody but me today. Well, not true—taking care of myself is just taking care of one corner of the universe; it's not selfish but responsible.

Light the lamp, figure out the e-mail machine. Ashley will get messages from many strings of the universe. All roads lead to Rome, and I'm on my way to Rome this time. It's on the way home to Mom. People came, and Gillian, the friend I will travel with this time. I listened to her and talked, and rested today—a slow sense of rightness that I have been blessed with the time to do it for me, to be here for her. It's not too late in the day to finish these pages; it's not too late in the day for anything, there is nothing I MUST do, nothing in the social schedule of how it should be, how I should fit in the world.

How did the divine manage to get me to this wonderful place? Grace. I must—I must—continue to listen, to move forward, sometimes slowly, sometimes with leaps, sometimes imperceptibly, to not react with anger or indignation, only watch the signs. My liver is off—why? Too fast too much? Not enough attention? I can feel better right away if I pay attention. If I know something is bad for me, don't do it, simply. Oh, a cool breeze. Look again at the castle drawings; leave them till later though. Put them in order and accessible, ready to go. Today actively rest, do small orderly things, readying things. Keep it simple. Write a book? Word by word, one idea at a time. Paint something, one stroke at a time. Go out and look at something—really look.

Wednesday

Get on track. Someone was singing in my dream—an overtone with him listening inside. His English was not fluent; it was a struggle. Also, he wanted the football game on television, but with the sound turned down because he was singing. We were talking about old boats, the Pinafore type. I was trying to go to the clinic for an operation—something small and insignificant—but put it off; it was too complicated to go and come back.

I hope that lizard didn't eat those dead ants, because there is poison; he will die too. Also, the birds...I will put them in the fire so no one will touch them. Ants are coming on me but they don't bite. Leave them be.

There's pressure around Siva. I told him to be very careful and quiet (inside); there is so much strong energy around these days, both disruptive and powerfully good. Choose, listen, be careful. I woke up with a bang, but at 4:30—too early. Mom is home in bed, but well. John is a bit distant—close that gap. Closed with a note. I must be able to eat today; I need the energy passing through me.

This pen is running out. It's a red one, kind of shocking—take it back to Desiderio. The only problem with writing so quickly is that I will never read it again. It doesn't matter, it's head-clearing. Start the day in a normal rhythm, if possible. It's already off—put it back in order. Finish this now—finish what I can, when I can—everything will fit together, all is in its place. The day is not overcrowded, there's lots of room for everything. Be an aboriginal, be a being, that's all, lose all the extra stuff. Have a bonfire—let it go, don't think about it, don't reflect, just let go—and then carry on, lighter, freer, happier. Simple.

Thursday
1 May

1. Keep lapis in your pocket.

2. Keep painting, in the mood or not; the mood will come.

Mom should keep painting, for her hips. Me too—paint, write, whatever. Keep the creativity flowing through. It is an energy. It is not OURS; if it gets blocked, it will hurt. What about the lady from New York—clothes full of light? Of course they should be. Can I go to Mom? I can go—a big trip with Gillian would be fun. We can do it. Get the Hyderabad castle commission; I can do it. Make the drawing today, colours with the architect. Colours with me, then tell him. Meet the lady at the Guest House. Press the shirts that I have, finish the white peacock dress (find the white peacock dress).

I feel better today. I feel well today: those are instructions for the body. The man in the market said, "You must reply, 'I am very well, thank you'—and then you will reply with the same question and [he] will say, 'Me too'—and then everyone will be better." Be shining—what joy to get everyone shiny, and keep them shiny—shine up everyone, cover you in light. Smile more of the time. Susan, start it— let light pour through. Whatever happens is an adventure, the challenge of life, each moment, each day. Ashley, I need to touch you. When can it fit in your life? Get there before he is in school. This year.

Friday
2 May

Oh, good morning—why good? Is it next to God? Might be. I'm reading too many books—or enough. Siva is here with me, like always, nothing strange; all the moments and months in between melted away. We both have changed, but also not at all. There is more to give. He is not going away even when he is not here in person. The feeling of being gathered in—taken rightfully, gently, without question—it's right, but such a soft thing. He is not soft and he is soft; I am also both those things. He IS a partner. Morning—leg is burning—a reminder. Care for it today. I cannot be crippled by care. Is the gardener here in the night? Did he see? It doesn't matter; only discretion, not hiding, is necessary.

No people today, no work people, only me, and Gillian. Travel with Gillian, she is a comrade in arms—and I am. My leg is bad, a bit; meditate over it, use the pendulum. Soothe the tendons, soothe the muscles, soothe the hip. Rest it, let it be well—let it be fully healthy. It was getting better. What I did wrong was only straining it—am I so readily inflamed? The motorcycle is also not great; it uses, a little, the same muscles. Don't be worried for Siva, or for me. Five months, we saw, we can manage our lives. We are all growing up—and not apart. I can breathe easier knowing everyone can cope.

Go to Mom this year, before school starts, while Ashley is a bit free. Check the dates—get to him, keep the touch of him—write copious letters to all of them. Hatch the plot to go, get the work rolling for that, to make it clear and easy. I am an artist. Be an artist in all of life, not just on paper. I was a little surprised at the neighbourhood shrink saying that yesterday. "You are an artist—been doing it for years. Keep going."

Saturday
2 May 97

Don't let the mind do so much talking before I get to the pen and paper. Talk talk talk before I open my eyes—Siva, the lawyer, Desiderio, and the waterfall noise of running water for hours with music behind. Mindless endless shower-taking, no idea how distracting it is. One neighbour complaining about another. We all make noise; this is a city. So many ties that bind me. Backache—is that why? Is it a looking-back ache? Village noise: they are chanting or shouting—chanting, but spoken—not restful noise. Roosters from there, birds twittering here, shrill brain fever bird, electricity on dim. I'm free today; I can write, paint what I want, organize cloth for Monday. Why, I wonder, are they shouting? Louder—it doesn't touch me but it does—maybe it's a happy thing. Maybe it's war. I'm so mixed up with all the sounds, the cacophony; don't let the noises get stuck in my head.

I will iron everything today. I can sit on the floor with it if I want. Lights are going up and down, not off, but I can't iron like this. Check if money doesn't come today; her intentions are good but I am pressed. Get the cloth for the pyramid before paying anything off. We need the money from that work to keep going—then it will be all right. Phone Madras clients, check the quilts (but one by one, or I will be overwhelmed). One thing at a time, slowly. Everything is all right.

Sunday
3 May 97

Clear out—from the dream. My hangings were every-where—I mostly was amazed by the coincidences of time and space. Get that pyramid done tomorrow, take it to Madras on Tuesday, check on our progress there. Check the e-mail from there. Clean the house. Get enough money to buy paper for painting. I'm looking at the painting work. The one from yesterday can be saved, I think. I was trying too much too fast. Concentrate on one thing at a time—too much and my attention wanders. Do a close-up, of anything: one leaf, one flower, one corner of a wall—catch the impulse for LOOKING. Concentrate. Remember that all the things I do well now, took years to grasp, in stages; cooking and sewing were well grounded in the small skills each step of the way till I forgot the years spent learning, because it was a pleasure. Do the exercises of painting first. Not for show. To learn. To understand what to do and why. I can see what I want to express, but I don't know how to arrive at it. Learn the techniques, then I can play with it freely. It's not difficult—relax, enjoy it, do the small exercises. Remember learning to type? How tedious and sometimes frustrating. Now that skill is in the fingers, by passing the struggling, mistake-laden mind. But I had to relax and trust myself to get to that point. There is really very little time that the calculating brain has to be in gear at all. My life is not about that. It is about precisely the other way: the trusting, joyful, intuitive way of living.

Monday
May 5

My mentor, why did we hurt each other so much? How she was holding onto me so hard—was I careless of her? I don't think so. I think a lot was buried below the surface. She was probably wise to back off and let me go so completely. If she had kept the tie so active I wouldn't have gone into this experience so fully. I feel like contacting her, but my solar plexus says NO, don't do it. Let her heal. Or what? Barge through the barrier anyway? She came all the way India to see me, no small matter. I will write—no troubles to give her, the adventure goes on. She had a big part in starting me off; I can touch gently (after all, if she is on this earth still, she would want to know). I want to know, how is she—was it too painful to look at my chart? Her name comes so often into my day. She should know that. I opened, I suppose, those channels by long-distance phone yesterday. Will I and Siva be all right? Yes—we must take care to gather our strength, to let the strength flow back. Keep open to light and health and power flowing in. Don't block it.

Dear Gillian, I see this is a bit hard for you, but I have enormous respect for the openness you are showing. The open heart- and minded-ness. Good girl. Today the pyramid canopy is the only real priority. Get it right, get it strong, put patches on the thing. Make it stronger. Relieve the stress at the corners. Consider how the pull is coming.

338

Don't add resistance, but fortify the strong parts. Explain that clearly—add support to the parts that get twisted, adjust the ties—of course they will come off if there is too much stress on one point. Clear the tangles. No confusion of pull in one spot.

Tuesday
6 May

We don't need to call the clairvoyant every ten minutes. He is a nice man and it's interesting—it helps in crunch times—but I don't need it. It's different to sit with a friend and discuss the aspects of life. Our own bootstraps. Go to Madras, do the work there, come home and get back to work. Make the things to stock for taking away. Be here for November. Go September/October. Ashley's birthday—check the machine this morning, find Ashley's phone number, talk to him. Dear Ashley, dear Ashley, dear Ashley, are you there? Yes, of course, I know you are. A letter is faster than e-mail for me—just write it and put in the box, it's easy. May June July August—enough under control to go. Get the visa straightened out. It's not yet run out. What has happened to the form? Get English books for Siva. Let him rise up—pull, no need to push. Thank you, thank him—me too—allow the rising up to happen like the sunrise. It doesn't matter if clouds are there; the rising still goes on even if I can't see it, and breaking through clouds makes beautiful patterns of light, beautiful colours. The whole cycle is like that—sunsets also, and comets, falling stars.

Wednesday 7

Squished in a bad mood. It doesn't matter if the pen has ink or not, I'm not going upstairs for another pen. Better do Bach flowers today. I'm afraid for Siva that he will fly off the edge—keep that together. Rescue Remedy everything— water, bath—can you rescue the laundry? Get that cough out of him—keep out of Desiderio's way. My head is ringing. But it's almost raining, also—what to do? All the right things: all the exercises, all the food, all the mantras. Get the chamber clear, take out the junk, take out the pile-up. First, neem tea. First, the cleaning—physical, emotional, mental—out out out all the mud possible, then work with what is left. Take care—me too. Make hot drinks; Siva is coughing deeply. He needs to feel better, needs to rest his body and mind. Make the neem, then finish the writing— for me too. OK, for the moment I have done all I can do; he is sleeping. He looks better than I did, because he has a clearer picture of the whole thing than I do; he KNOWS what he has to go through, he knows the consequences.

All I can do is stand back, let go of the pictures in my head, light the lamps, do the chores, be all right. Make an invoice for Madras, ask for what I need (figure out first what I need), just clear this mud and have my bath—clearing,

clearing—slow down—slow down, stop going in circles. One steady straight line—maybe it goes around, but aim straight, take one slow step at a time. Clean up, clear out. Get everything ready for the commission work, make a plan for the pyramid. See exactly what we need to finish it. Keep quiet—get quiet. Take my bath, get clean—stay clean. Sweep inside and outside aura—house, everything, even the bugs from the porch. Sweeping sweeping sweeping sweeping sweeping sweeping.

Thursday 8

I'm stuck this morning—fever in the house, and rain will come again. At 8:15 I will go to phone the lawyer again—see if I have all the papers. The tea water is hot. A lot of pressure is there; don't resist. Let this pass over, let it pass through. It's not the kind to fight against. Nothing to fight. Let it go through. Rest more. Do an invoice for a client going travelling with my work. If she isn't clear about where she is going, she won't sell extra things. It's clear that she has the need but not the push. It's Thursday; call the Hyderabad architect in two more days. Siva's house is empty; is he empty? Almost—a hard hard time. Don't let him go out. Stay here resting, with salts, brewer's yeast, vitamin B. What about me? I got used to being alone in the house. He needs time to find energy.

Every house in the neighbourhood is disrupted by some-thing or other right now. Desiderio? Hard to say, maybe. Always hanging on by a thread—the thread with lapis stone? Don't get confused today. Last week it felt like we were so much all together; now it feels like we are so much alone. But the threads are there, trust is there. We can move to each other; the base is there for everyone to do what they need to do and there is a net.

Bring that fever down, clean the room, put the machine somewhere, wash the cloth, pack the things going to Europe. Put the canopy away, organize Siva's clothes. Remind him that there is a closet. Fix the lamps, or at least one of them. Make the bed, check the fever, get enough food, take something to drink, make tea, hot bath, everything with Rescue Remedy, brewer's yeast for both of us. Clean also upstairs, make a mat for here, downstairs little quilted ones for the feet at the door, for under the cushion also. Renew everything possible: blood, body, cushion covers. Get neat; straighten everything—affaires réglés, affaires réglés, affaires réglés.

Friday
9 May

Okay, I've sorted out the day and date—now my head. Work for Siva. Keep him busy, involved. Can we do the Philodendron quilt over again? Change the thread? Then I can sell it if we need to—the first bird one also. Just keep one here at a time. Check with the Boutique. Write to Ashley. Sweet of him to send a Mother's Day card—sweet peas. The air is different today; is it because of the police all round for the vice-president? Can I pull through this time? Remember the waves of feelings from before, stay really quiet—let them go over, let them pass through (also me), keep moving and walk away from the mud. Don't get stuck in the mud. Go to Canada when it is time. The world will not fall apart when I do that. Everything will keep moving.

Saturday 10

Photocopies should be done by a stranger. I dreamed of Ashley just now; there are three times he can come this year, three possibilities: June, September, November. Today I have to find money. Please—for Raju, Jyothi, Gillian, me—the cheque should come. My other commissions should come through. Pendulum, rune stones—there is no need for me to be struggling with money anymore. I don't want to be held back by that. Keep moving—gently.

Monday

OK, go! Pull the plug, talk now. All the silly things wanting space acknowledged—come forth! Look how lazy I'm being, drifting around in my mind, lapsing completely, daydreaming. Siva, the difference between trust and faith.

He had something else to do; it's good that he went and did it instead of staying here and worrying—and worrying me. Oh, Siva didn't come today—I think he has gone to Cuddalore—I hope he doesn't blow this thing. This part in his story is his karma; mine is to stay quiet and not be upset. What about my visa? I think the form is just underway (check with the visa service). Incoming: Rs. 4,700 + 7,100 + 10,000 + 11,000 = 32,800. To go out: taxi 2,000 – cloth 8,000 – Siva 5,000 – Pour Tous account 5,000 – Pondy cloth 2,000 = 22,000. Wages 3 x 2,500 – incoming 2,000.

Balance = 9,000 – 2,000 (some to go to Madras) = 7,000 – 2,000 for Siva's bank = 5,000 left over. There, we are all right; I am all right, nothing to worry about. Keep working, keep plugging away. Be open to the small things coming in; it will add up to be enough—more than enough. Go see the new client's house with her this week, make the slip for her, do all the little work, be prepared for the big one coming. Quilt shop in Canada—write again to them (maybe they didn't even get my letter), get things moving. Keep some money in hand for safety—not hoarding—just keep some to cover what has to be done, don't spend it before you've got it. Be ready to cycle to the bank, be ready to take one canopy to the gallery, be ready to do everything, but not just anything. Write to the architect—maybe the estimate is high? Of course it is—I wasn't supposed to do that work. I did the estimate like it was a one time wonder, a wonderful thing. Yes, I was generous on all sides. I won't change it; it wasn't a mistake. Fully paint a gardenia today, even this morning. Be ready for the new gallery in Pondy. Three metres or 3.2 makes a big difference. Yes, we can do the flowers.

Wednesday
May 14

Losing days, but not lost. Better to get up and write than get up and read. I can read after. I noticed by chance on Monday that I did four pages, not three. My mind is full still. I became sad yesterday for Siva—for me. Don't lose heart; it will be all right. Keep heart, be good—he must be lost, or maybe found. Halfway between here and his house—but which house? I had lost any thought of him going back to that place—to prison, to jail. Please don't make him go back, please. So much misunderstanding, so much bad difficult feeling, so much confusion and so much clarity and strength. So much power and joy, so much love and so much beauty and grace to be thankful for. So many good things, so many miracles. Such protection from going off the path. So many good people, so many abundant miracles. So much help is there. So many things to be thankful for.

My home is here, freely. My peacock is here, my friends are here (new good ones), my brother is being so good. John. Desiderio is giving me so much so freely. Cast my mind around. Anyone faced directly is facing directly in return. I can learn to paint. My house is full of silk and beautiful things. I got a lovely note and flowers yesterday, and fruit from the gardener. My mother is there—I will go. My Ashley—was I dreaming he will come? Maybe? I will go to him. My sisters—pray they are all right. They are good sisters. Desiderio's mother is waiting in Paris to hear the signal words - affaires règles. All is well and I'm getting a real chance to learn that. Nothing to complain about, nothing at all. All is in its place in the universe.

Thursday 15

Too much sun—ache through kidneys. Money is tight. Add it up—it will be all right. The pressure of Siva, money, in the house, in the air. He stopped cold, mind looking at his brother's new motorbike. A loan for that, but not for this. What to do? I suppose he is right—this is not his problem, in a way. I think he is already taking a load. Invent more clothes; invent a longer kurta. Phone Madras clients, write to Canada, follow the leads that are leading in the right direction. Get tofu. Get ready to do the work, get ready to finish off everything. Put what I have in action, wash the one from the Boutique. Work on a drawing, tie the knots on the quilts—it will take days, a nice work. Caftans—black handwoven cotton and linen, black and tussar silk bamboo design, if there is enough.

Keep love in the world. Write write write—can I write a book about this experience that will touch people in a way that is helpful—to me, or to one person in the world who is struggling in this way? Or to Ashley, because I haven't been able to write letters during this time, to tell him clearly how I feel—to pass something on to my son (all the sons). We don't just get shelved into a role of Mother and sit around being only that. The children must surpass, must go further, higher than we have. It can help if they know clearly what it is they came from—what struggles, or what look like struggles. Why we looked like we were acting as we did, what is behind that: the warrior as a mother.

Friday
16 May 97

Because afterwards I can't tell one year from another. If I can't remember the date at the library or now, for instance, how am I expected to remember after any length of time? Change the bed today. Bring the one from downstairs up. I am not a martyr. Or maybe I have been, but stop it. Ask for help with phone bill money.

What are those ants doing? Something must have expired; follow the trail back. It's just a bigger bug, and they are taking it outside. I'm so upset about the tofu—why? All the coming and going is all right, that people were confused and told me the wrong thing is also okay, but to be accused of being there at the wrong time, when that's what I was told, is not okay. She did soften a bit. I could see she was busy, probably making mango chutney (which is my favourite thing). Oh, what next. John was right, I forgot it is May; it is warmer than I think. How was she to know—why should she—that all the other things are pressing?

Look at the paintings. I like the little leaf of yesterday. And the hibiscus is too small, too much in the middle, but the background is interesting to me—not completely tasteful but a good experiment in wet on wet. Got a new notebook in Madras. Deliver things to be delivered. Just go and come back. Try to stay calm, try to stay cool and relaxed. I think the lawyer doesn't believe Siva. The new papers must show something. Let him do what he has to do. This part is not my work. I will not drop it, but help has to be there now. I do not want to die from this tension. Someone to look at my hip—what is going on in there? Or it will disappear; it is going, but why so long? Change the bed. This one is like lying on the floor. Soft would be good. Softer.

5:00 a.m.
Saturday
17 May 97

Spiders are very fast—I cross their threads on my way downstairs—how long would it take them to fill up the house? I forgot to make the invoice; remember now to take it with me to Madras. I can do it with her there, just take the file in my bag. I woke up, "Why am I having to do these things now?" which is why I set the alarm for 5:00 (it went off at 4:45; alarms are very independent things, minds of their own, I think). Runes said just be quiet, do not collapse into emotions, blockages at the beginning of a new life, nourish the wellspring. There will be more than enough to look after everyone. But first me.

Maybe we can finish the big canopy before Thursday. Will I have Siva? Who knows—only God. I only want this thing cleared up, because the strain is heavy, but hasn't it been interesting to have to plumb that deep, to let the pain pass. How will he be if he has to go back? What was the lawyer trying to tell me? It wasn't necessary to bring Siva; it's not in my hands, not in my control. There's nothing I can do for him now except hold the fort, take care of myself, carry on carrying on, be open to the new direction, try to pay my bills. Don't worry about a thing; don't sweat the small stuff. When you can't fight and you can't flee, flow. Take cushions in the car and rest when I can. Take a neem branch. Remember that the divine is at hand. Don't use canvas on the umbrella; use the heavy polyester, and use Velcro strips so it can be replaced when necessary. Keep it light, let the light come through, use the light yellow. Let it be airy, let it be free, let the sun come in softly. It may be soft but it is strong. Let it shine in—the light.

Sunday
18 May 97

Oh, hot sweet tea. Why so often do I get sorted out by going on the road? The hours of sitting still. Hot wind, solid and smooth, warm on my skin like being touched on purpose. Nothing to do but sit still and enjoy it. Dear Mr. R, we both left you yesterday much quieted, in a good way. It is something that is getting worked on constantly. It's too bad that people normally meet their lawyer under stressful conditions. But maybe not—I saw us each able to grab hold again of the calm quiet place. Siva told me that he was much reassured by the things you said. He had made a list of points and questions and you brought each one of them up yourself. We didn't rehash the whole meeting.

The day before, we had each separately been struck with one of the waves of fatigue and questioning. Why me, why this experience? It was heavy, and each of us stayed very quiet and didn't move (he in Madras and me here in Auroville), and then it turned into something else. The black ages at the beginning of a new life, the gift of a time like this to see that the divine is close at hand, the chance to "not panic" (it's easy not to panic when there is nothing pressing—or maybe not; human beings love to make drama). But, as you say, it's much more fun to try to be above that. There has even been a lot of joy in the past few years, when I ALLOW it to come: the joy that arises from facing the situation, the wonder of the real support (divine and human) through THAT real frustration, and anger and sadness to overcome. Real enemies to stand firm for, and the fight melts away. There is no fight—only this glowing chance to grow.

BURGUNDY DAY-TIMER DIARY (1998)

3 January 98

Rs 200 Balance to Raju

Rs. 400 Cuddalore Court: Raju, Jyothi

Rs. 300 Advance Jyothi

Rs. 2000 Siva Loan

Rs. 300 Villipuram Trip

7 January 98

Phone call to the lawyer

9 January 98

Dentist

Pondy Boutique

Jyothi, Cuddalore Court

14 February 98

Runes asking for Radical Trust

3 March 98

#15 Court Hall – High Court, Madras 10:30–1:00

Tuesday
17 March 98

Phone Quiet Healing Centre, Watsu treatment

Rajaram Taxi

Lawyer address: Ashok Nagar

Inner Ring Road

Opposite New Telephone Exchange

Art Supply List:

Aquarelle Arches (56 x 76 cm)	185 lbs	Rs. 126
Grain fin	185lbs	Rs.126

Madras (Siva)

#15 Court Hall

High Court

19 March 98

Runes

Breakthrough

Growth: go deeply with care and awareness. Flow of beings into new forms, gentle action, disperse resistance and rectification carried out, holding firm. With steadfastness and the right attitude, blossoming can occur.

Radical discontinuity.

25 March 98

Court

1 April 98

LAST COURT

Bail granted.

Madras with in-laws.

But one more affidavit, one more court.

3 April 98

Villipuram Sessions Court

Rs. 10,000 on account

Bail papers, evening

Saturday
4 April 98

Raju picked up papers in Madras.

Tuesday
7 April 98

Finally, the coded message to Paris:

> SIVA – affaire réglée

20 AUGUST 98 (11:00 A.M.)

Thursday. If I concentrate, this can reach you by your birthday.

Thursday: fish day. John for dinner. I don't always feel like cooking fish—I'm sure you understand—but the boost is good. John is so darn appreciative, and thinks it's so much work (what, it takes three minutes), so...

It was funny to open your letter and be faced with pictures of ME. I took a magnifying glass to all your works in progress. We are CLOSE to getting up the energy to paint again after the summer.

Aside: Plumeria still blooming a little.

We are doing a nice bit of work just now. A woman here who is making a new house pushed and pulled until I finally caved in and agreed to make curtains for her bedroom. I wouldn't have relented except that the design popped into my mind.

Anyway, the work's fun, in the way that a good solid project that you can get your teeth into for a couple of weeks is.

I've just now finished MY part—it's all cut out.

3:30 DONE. Fresh start tomorrow with stitching.

Tomorrow has arrived! Siva is upstairs humming along (actually).

I was Summoned today. The Secretary (gov't type) of the AV Foundation's WIFE wanted to meet me; she needs clothes. I ended up staying for lunch. I hadn't met them before. Nice and interesting people.

Before being attached to Auroville, he had been the executive director of the Handloom Export Promotion Council. He knows ALL about cloth—loves it—and is ready to share.

(We're going to phone you on your birthday.)

BULLETIN: I feel like I have received evidence that there is, in fact, Divine Grace.

The "woman who has been my major antagonist over the last four years" story. I was in the cafeteria at the Information Centre. She just started working there. It was quiet. I was in line behind a couple of visitors taking things to go. Then we were alone in the place. I was concentrating the whole time on not sending out any aggression or putting up any defences. To be quiet enough inside to let her find some peace with herself, however many years that was going to take.

She turned and walked away into the kitchen without acknowledging I was there at all. I stayed quiet. Right away another woman came and took my request (tea, of course). I stayed nice. Soft. Not pretending.

Moments later she came to me. She must have been so scared—she touched me on the shoulder and when I turned she said, "I'm sorry—are you all right?" "Yes," I told her, "and thank you."

You hardly ever saw such a smile of relief, hers.

A small event, but a major victory.

*****

New topic: I haven't really lost weight either, just compacted. But now perhaps I've gained a pound or two. I'm not quite so frighteningly skinny. Also, now that Siva has been back for a while, I am looking more relaxed, and therefore younger. And on top of that, I am getting in the mood to let my hair grow. Obviously it IS growing, and there is a GOOD hairdresser who can help the process happen gracefully.

I seem to be telling all the "little" things, but my hand isn't sweating and there's time.

NEW DELHI: I've scratched it, for now. The trigger was that the lady on that end got sidetracked; she flew off to Chicago for ten days, stuff like that. She still wants me to come, but I had begun to see that it's been a long stretch that

I haven't really been able to work properly RIGHT HERE. Trials and tribulations, hip mood out, basically worn out.

Finally I am beginning to have solid energy again. I don't want to just spill it, to waste it. We will spend this season working solidly and see what can happen when the whole crew is present and accounted for—and ready to work!

I know also that I will be making the grand attempt to get there to you. The plot is underway. I have said it out loud and started planning to myself.

*****

Wow! What a gorgeous sight. I was gazing out the window—a late afternoon sun shower, with (heavy) glorious light. Fading fast, but inspiring.

*****

Definite shift in the weather. A cover at night (well, not all night), and the morning cool bath, which normally feels like it's completely OK—no thought of a shock—this morning I wanted to resist pouring the water down my back.

...to be continued...

but RIGHT NOW I'M GOING TO POST this.

with very much love

as always

Susan

Sunday something
September 98

French keyboqrd, remember (read "a" zhen you often see "q," and "m" when you see "," that doesn't seem to be in the right place.

Now I not only have to scramble for the e-mail, but Siva is taking typing classes every day for the next zhile (also, "z" is in "w's" spot).

The new project is SILK SCREEN! I am about to produce the DESIGNER LUNGI! Brilliant. I am so excited at this concept; it must be rather the same fqscinqtion qs your cards. Many of my drawings, of course, will work qlmost qs they are and I have had the first one scanned on the computer. It is on the floppy disk and down at the place in Pondy to be put on a photographic screen. I am having to learn everything, and the first step seems to be finding out exactly what it is I have to learn. I think it isn't complicated, just a matter of getting at it. But we hzve begun! My head is surging with possible applications, seems never-ending. I know that the world has been silk screening forever, but it's just grabbed ahold of me. I will continue the other work, but can branch out in this way on the side (should, could actually turn out to be major). I'm sure you quickly grasp the thrill that it isn't so labour intensive, also.

Tonight is chicken day. Last time that happened on a Sunday I ended up feeding everyone around, including

John. Ready for him to show up for his Sunday tea and get tempted.

We are not having the tourist season that normally happens; the only reassuring thing is that I don't think we are having a tighter time than anyone else. Not starving, don't worry. When I speak with friends who also have small working groups we are still grateful that we HAVE small groups, and aren't under the burden of some huge overhead and can easily adjust.

How is your new bionic hip? Are you having pain? I do hope it's all relieved.

I have told the physio that I'm aiming at being Superwoman. He says it will take a little while. Got a little spunky this week and did some gardening after work; the weather is nigh on perfect from five to six o'clock in the evening, and then it gets dark quickly. Pulled one too many weeds, but it's so tempting now that it's raining on and off and the ground is a little softer, and at the same time every-thing starts to grow like mad. I think every seed that fell to earth during the summer just waits to spring into action.

Try not to worry. You have been a good and excellent mother all along the way.

love, S

14 September 98

Here I am at typing school with Siva. He is getting the first row down pat. Now the girl teacher is checking that I can, in fact, type. I will have to be careful what I say because I think she is going to stay with me. She is a pretty girl, also pretty interested in me. That made her smile and even blush.

I told you yesterday about our new project; I now think there is one MORE. That one has to be kept under wraps until confirmed. It will be worth an e-mail.

I had a good letter from Ashley today. He is figuring out how to manage his feelings about his other grandmother passing. They were away and missed the funeral, he had just read the eulogy. He seems to be opening and warming. Not much residue of the tension from last fall. Maybe all gone. I think he understood something after we went through that. All human beings.

We have driven all the way into Pondy to this school. Siva has been coming every day, and invited me to come with him to check it out and look at the difference between this machine and the French keyboard at home. I think he just wanted company.

Yes, I had the whole neighbourhood for dinner. John was smiling and said, "Just think, we can look back in twenty years and remember the days when we used to come to Susan's café." Desiderio replied, "What do you mean? We still will be doing it."

This is a huge old heavy manual machine and my fingers are going to get tired if I have to keep this up to impress this girl standing by me checking me for mistakes. Yup, she is laughing.

We girls will start drawing and painting again on Thursday, now that people are back from their summer roaming. Our small group will attempt to be relaxed and strict with ourselves at the same time. I suppose the word is discipline.

We won't get our art teacher this winter to help us; I think she has an exhibition at the UN. It means some pretty serious preparation. She was just in Scotland doing the art therapy part of a workshop run by the woman that I stayed with on Maui. Then back to Italy and Colorado in October. I don't know how she arrived at the fantasy of getting back to Auroville this year.

It looks like I have more time on this machine. I will tell you about the proposed proposal of this morning. Full-fantasy sort of work. OK, first think of the Wizard of Oz in that big room inside wherever it was. Now, this place is to be a Temple of World Peace—it's actually being built in Madras, by one of the half dozen or so wealthiest families in India (means rich). The place that needs decorating is white marble, of course, and it seams (oh, the tailor in me) seems they want twelve pairs of cloth panels, which will open somehow electronically as the Wizard arrives. Each pair of panels should be about seven metres high and ten wide. Yup!

All white and sheer. I have the plot, already since this morning, of how to do it, with designs of a flame (central thought in the place), but all in white. I have estimated the cloth at about two thousand metres. How long it will take to make? About seventeen man weeks. The cost will be enough to solve all my crunches. They want to open in November. There would be about eight weeks to complete the thing. If everyone works like mad, we CAN do it!

I'm busy making positive formations. The architect who they are talking to about the decoration phase of this project is talking only to me, so if THEY get it, I get it too.

It's so much fun to think of doing really big things. We were both so excited this morning in his office, declaring we LOVE BIG THINGS!

Actually, the nicest part is simply the feeling of being happy—seeing the creative part of my mind in full action. Again.

Sometimes I got worried that it might have got stomped out over the past few years—too much serious time, too much discomfort physically, to feel like dreaming up ideas. Such joy when they can just come rolling again. I know you understand that, even to FEEL like sitting up long enough to draw or paint, or never mind that even, to be able to take full pleasure from a really good book without being distracted by something aching.

Ah, 5:50 (1750 hrs;). School almost out. I should come more often. Captive at a typewriter!

I've impressed the teacher. We know that I can type very fast. But I've made her day. It's good she's gone; they also get amazed at left-handedness.

25 September 98

The last instalment for this envelope.

I have submitted my drawings—white on white translucent paper, a series—these people need all the help at visualizing they can get!

The architect went yesterday. They loved it. He will go again this weekend to confirm the whole parcel and GET MONEY.

We are, as a group, trying to remain detached and not mind whichever way it goes.

Actually, it means I am getting caught up on all sorts of other things.

I'm also teaching a friend this way of quilting. A nice project. We are making her do everything herself, of course—finally today she is cutting the cloth! Fun to watch her.

6 October 98

Oh, I'm so bad— but the quilt is done! We helped, of course. The NEXT one is all hers.

That was also the last page in the pad. We (me) were really busy, spent a week or so doing drawings for the Madras bunch (WHITE on TRANSPARENT paper), bit of Emperor's new clothes feeling. Everyone, including client, loved it, BUT I don't think the whole thing will happen. It seems these fabulously wealthy types play a lot of games (we know that already).

It leaves me room to get back to the other brainstorms— a good time for work.

RAIN—this has all been written during that kind of weather. The newspaper today says it's over! Except that that was the SUMMER MONSOON—LATE—and the WINTER MONSOON is on its way—EARLY.

I hope there's time for the laundry to dry.

I'm making a resolution to MAIL LETTERS to you as I do each chapter.

I will try very hard.

Always love
Susan

Siva just came back from school this moment. Jayaram is coming for dinner too, walking more easily on his new leg! And I'm getting smarter; I have discovered that he can pick up dinner TO GO on his way home!

xoxoxoxxo

How's the TOTEM coming along?!

21 November 98

This is typed on the back of an enlarged photocopy (rejected because it's off the edge) of a drawing that has been scanned on the computer, then printed.

The object of this game is to be able to make use of the wonderful new "machine" (a plotter, I think it is called) that should be able to enlarge anything to almost any size once they figure out exactly how to use it. I've got them all jumping through hoops, and we are all figuring out what it is we have to learn in order to even START—but they are playing because we are ALL going to need it, or be able to dream up a use.

This morning itself I delivered to the silk-screening man the enlarged photocopy to turn into screens, and also the cloth to make the first experiments. I still had to do progressive photocopy enlargements because the program isn't quite the compatible one yet. Next week.

Yes, that was long and drawn-out, but it has been. Even this morning the poor young man was reporting a fever of 102, but I was tough, and said, "It will pass—four, five days, had that one."

Your letter was thought-provoking, I was thinking about you being my age now when you moved to Pender Island, and Ashley about the same age now as John was (for you) when he came here. John and I were looking at these things from all the angles we could think up the other night. Getting new slants on each other's thoughts and feelings—yours, mine, his.

I think it's good to be fifty.

I finally got a little smart. I bought a new APPLIANCE (Rs. 24). It's a LONG BROOM. I do mean long. The skinny handle is about eight feet, with a little tuft of coconut fibre on the top. It's for the ceiling, spider webs and things. You can imagine my joy and smugness when suddenly I could simply reach. Been eyeing these brooms for years, but it's not obvious how to get them home from the market on a motorcycle. The traffic you remember.

YES, you could manage a light touch machine. Those things are FUN. You can type anywhere: on the couch, in bed, on the ferry. They don't make hardly any noise at all, and they are FASTER and effortless. More like a game than work.

We are doing some nice projects right now, a bit of a line-up, actually. Mostly using a handloom cotton that I have used on and off for years. Good colours, texture, tough, easy to work with. Suddenly everyone NEEDS big hanging curtains. And probably three new houses that I will just get to play in. Lovely. Meanwhile, apparently working capital (good-sounding words, huh?) is in the mail from Bombay, toward preparation for that joint show in April.

You see, the hard time is getting over with. I will send photos of the coat that went to Connecticut via Gillian (the coat went with her, film is still in the camera).

I'm still jealous of your "Mother Bear" carving project for your community hall, but I am going to do a silk screen of the totem design that I made some time ago so that I will be with you in my own way.

John is well, still working evenings with solar bowl mirrors. They will be done soon. I seem to be feeding him more often these days. We're keeping his energy up.

So, if he didn't write lately, forgive him. But I will ask him if he did. Always with love, and to my sisters, both.

Susan

AFTERWARD

The next months were full of preparation for Bombay in the spring. I did go. Siva came too.

And then invitations, accepted, for an earth circling round of trunk shows, that let me arrive at my Canadian West Coast destination in time for the Millennium gathering with my Pender Island community.

I knew when I embarked for Australia, flying in the opposite direction from my Canadian family that there were fresh shadows, serious illnesses on that side. I felt sickened too, that I had to fly off and celebrate with friends on the way. But those exhibitions would pay my fares, and many other things. So, Madras, Sydney, New York, Florida, Sante Fe, Vancouver.

When I arrived in Canada, it became clear without doubt that I was needed more in the West, for now. I made a quick trip back to Auroville, to arrange what I could, work for my team, and start out again with another plane ticket that would allow me the longest stay possible in Canada. It wasn't a happy leaving. It wasn't convenient. It was my path.

*****

I've come to the beach now to think over that last year. I was happy, sad, exhausted, from our long and lonely trial. There was no automatic instant sense of rosiness. I tried to be gentle with all of us. My other boys too, had worked so hard to do their part in helping us all to survive.

I am still in Canada.